EMBRACING LATINA SPIRITUALITY

Embracing Latina Spirituality

A

WOMAN'S

PERSPECTIVE

Michelle A. Gonzalez

ST. ANTHONY MESSENGER PRESS
Cincinnati, Ohio

Scripture passages have been taken from *New Revised Standard Version Bible*, copyright
©1989 by the Division of Christian Education of the National Council of the Churches
of Christ in the U.S.A., and used by permission. All rights reserved.

Book and cover design by Mark Sullivan
Cover image ©jupiterimages.com/Edward Duarte

LIBRARY OF CONGRESS CATALOGING-IN-PUBLICATION DATA
Gonzalez, Michelle A.
Embracing Latina spirituality : a woman's perspective / Michelle A. Gonzalez.
p. cm.
Includes bibliographical references (p.   ) and index.
ISBN 978-0-86716-886-0 (pbk. : alk. paper) 1. Hispanic American women—Religious
life. 2. Hispanic American Catholics—Religious life. I. Title.
BX1407.H55G658 2009
248.8'4308968073—dc22
2008052282

ISBN 978-0-86716-886-0

Published by St. Anthony Messenger Press
28 W. Liberty St.
Cincinnati, OH 45202
www.SAMPBooks.org
www.CalledtoHoliness.org

Printed in the United States of America.

Printed on acid-free paper.

09 10 11 12 5 4 3 2 1

CONTENTS

I wish to acknowledge the support and encouragement of an organization of philanthropists: Foundations and Donors Interested in Catholic Activities (FADICA). In January of 2005, I was invited to speak before this organization at a conference entitled Women of Faith. The discussion explored the many contributions of women to Roman Catholic ministry, church leadership and theology.

The members of FADICA heard my appeal for a renewed focus on women's spirituality in the context of significant religious change during the twentieth century and the pressing challenges of the twenty-first. The need for a creative, solidly grounded, and theologically sophisticated spirituality available in an accessible form for all Christian women seemed obvious. Follow-up conversations by the FADICA board, ably led by Frank Butler, led to a proposal from Fairfield University for a series of books on women's spirituality. Thus, FADICA, Fairfield University, and St. Anthony Messenger Press formed a collaborative partnership to produce seven volumes under the title *Called to Holiness: Spirituality for Catholic Women*.

I wish to thank individuals and foundations whose generosity made this collaborative venture possible. These include the Amaturo Family Foundation, the AMS Fund, the Cushman Foundation, the Mary J. Donnelly Foundation, George and Marie Doty, Mrs. James Farley, the Robert and Maura Burke Morey Charitable Trust, Maureen O'Leary, Ann Marie Paine and the Raskob Foundation for Catholic Activities. I wish to extend a word of thanks and praise to the entire FADICA membership, whose conscientious, quiet and loving participation in shaping the life of the church has been an inspiration.

*The focus of this series is spirituality. Its interest is women of all back-*grounds: rich and poor; married and single; white, black and brown; gay and straight; those who are biological mothers and those who are mothers in other senses. There will be volumes on grassroots theology, family life, prayer, action for justice, grieving, young adult issues, wisdom years and Hispanic heritage. I hope all the volumes in this series will deepen and shape your own spiritual life in creative ways, as you engage with the theology of our rich, two-thousand-year-old Christian tradition.

Women's spiritualities are lived in light of their concrete, specific experiences of joy and struggle; ecstasy and despair; virtue and vice; work and leisure; family and friends; embodiment and sexuality; tears and laughter; sickness and health; sistering and mothering. These volumes are for women and men from all walks of life, whether they are new to the spiritual journey or old hands, affluent, middle-class or poor. Included in the circle we call church are persons from every country on the planet, some at the center, others at the margins or even beyond.

The time is ripe for "ordinary" women to be doing theology. The first and second waves of the women's movement in the nineteenth and twentieth centuries provided a valiant and solid foundation for the third wave which will mark, and be marked by, the world of the early twenty-first century. Changes and developments from one generation to the next makes our heads spin. Younger women readers are likely to be already grooming the soil for a fourth wave of Christian spirituality done by and for women. Women have always loved God, served others and struggled with sin, but the historical context has been less than friendly in terms of women's dignity, acknowledgment of female gifts and empowerment by church and society. In a time of growing emphasis on the role of clergy, and the backlash against women in society, the voices of the laity—especially the voices of women—are needed more than ever.

The Greek language has two words for time. *Chronos* points to the time signaled by the hands on the clock—for example, it is a quarter past two. *Kairos* points to time that is ripe, a moment pregnant with possibility. As Christian women, we live in a time rightly described as *kairos*. It is a time that calls us, demands of us renewed energy, reflection and commitment to attend to and help each other grow spiritually as we seek to love ourselves and the world. At this point in history, the fruit of women's struggle includes new self-awareness, self-confidence and self-respect. More and more women are beginning to see just how lovable and capable they are. The goal of the Christian life has always been to lay down our lives in love for the other, but the particular ways this vocation is lived out differ from era to era and place to place. Women's ability to voice with confidence the phrase, "I am a theologian" at the beginning of the twenty-first century means something it could not have meant even fifty years ago.

Those who were part of the early waves of feminism celebrate the hard-won accomplishments of the women's movement and know that this work needs to be taken up by future generations. Young women in their twenties and thirties are often unaware of past efforts that brought about more dignity and freedom for women. Women have opened many doors, but many remain closed. The media have recently explored the plight of Hindu widows in India; less publicized is that women in the United States still earn only seventy-seven cents for every dollar earned by their male counterparts. We must be vigilant and continue to act for decades to come in order to secure our accomplishments thus far and make further inroads toward the creation of a just, egalitarian world. Those who sense that the women's movement is in a doldrums inspire us to renew the enthusiasm and dedication of our foremothers.

When we cast our eye beyond the women of our own nation, it takes but a split-second to realize that the majority of the world's poor and oppressed are women. A quick visit to the Women's Human Rights Watch Web site reveals the breadth and depth of women's oppression across the globe from poverty and domestic abuse to sex slavery. Most women (and their children) do not have enough to eat, a warm, dry place to sleep or access to education. Female babies are more at risk than male babies. Women, more than men, lack the protection of the law and the respect of their communities. The double-standard in sexual matters affects women in harmful ways in all cultures and economic groups across the globe.

For all of these reasons it is not just important—but pressing, crucial, urgent—that all women of faith own the title "theologian" and shape this role in light of each woman's unique set of characteristics, context, relationships and spiritualities. We are theologians when we sort through our experience and the great and small problems of our time through reflection on Scripture or the words of a mystic or theologian. The images of God that emerged for Paul, Augustine or Catherine of Siena provide guidance, but their theology cannot ever be a substitute for our own. Theology helps us shape what we think about God, justice, love, the destiny of humanity and the entire universe in a way that is relevant to the specific issues facing us in the twenty-first century. The call to spiritual depths and mystical heights has never been more resounding.

Elizabeth A. Dreyer
Series Editor

Community and Communion

As a teenager I often struggled with negotiating between my parents' very traditional Cuban cultural values and my progressive United States sensibilities. It always seemed unfair to me that my social life was hindered by their stricter worldview; they seemed to view the smallest bit of freedom as somehow scandalous. I will never forget their parting words each time I would be on my way out the door, liberated to this or that party or gathering: "Don't embarrass *us*," not "Don't embarrass *yourself.*" That subtle change in pronoun made a world of difference, reminding me that I was part of a larger whole, that my identity was ultimately wedded to my family's and that I was a representative of our clan to the world.

I often teach in the area of Latina theology, and two themes I always mention as foundational for understanding Latina identity and spirituality are community and family. It is no accident that the most significant film made in the United States about the Latina community is entitled *Mi Familia.* Starring actors including Jennifer Lopez and Jimmy Smits, this 1995 Gregory Nava film traces three generations of Mexican-American families and the struggles they confront in the United States. The film demonstrates a central concern for Latina culture and spirituality: family and community. Latinas share a communal worldview in which the individual is not understood as isolated and independent but exists in a web of communal and familial relationships. In other words, for Latinas, the individual is always interdependent. Who we are is intimately linked to our families, and families are not just the typical nuclear unit of parents and children, but include extended families and even close friends. Often Latinas refer to folks as *tía* and *tío* (aunt and uncle) who are not even relatives. This familial worldview permeates Latina religious beliefs and practices and is the foundation of Latina spirituality. Latinas, as the traditional gatekeepers and transmitters of Latina faith and religion, place this communal, familial understanding of their relationship with the sacred at the center of their spiritual beliefs and practices. For non-Latinas, Latina spirituality offers a communally oriented sense of identity and religiosity that is a fresh alternative to the individualism that permeates the dominant culture of the United States.

Latinas' emphasis on community as a fundamental dimension of our identity is a key contribution to Catholic women's spirituality. Who we are cannot be reduced to an isolated "I" but must instead be understood as an "I" that is organically linked to a collective "we." My identity is intimately linked to that of my parents, grandparents, husband and children. I cannot understand who I am without reflecting on these relationships and how they shape and affect me. The same is true for the Latina understanding of our relationship with the sacred. Latinas have a very interpersonal and reciprocal spirituality. This is seen particularly in our popular religion. The sacred is treated in ways that are similar to the ways we treat the people we encounter in our lives. We have conversations with our statues of saints and Mary, we leave them flowers and light candles in order to persuade them to gain favor for us and we become angry with them when our prayers are not answered. While this may seem irreverent, it is not. Instead, it offers a refreshing spiritual alternative that non-Latinas can also embrace. In treating Mary, the saints and even Jesus as our family members and friends, we are embracing a non-hierarchical spirituality.

The focus of this text is Latina spirituality. However, I hope the reader does not approach this book in a detached manner—as an outsider might study an "other" group. For the non-Latina reader, this book serves as a window into a particular Roman Catholic spirituality which I hope will help inform your own spiritual life. One does not have to be a Latina in order to light a candle to Our Lady of Guadalupe. Latinas who read this text will likely find some stories, narratives and analyses that mirror their own spirituality. They will also find ones that do not. After all, even though we are grouped under one broad category, we Latinas are a diverse lot. Because my audience is the broader community of Roman Catholic women, in this introductory section I begin by linking Latina spirituality to this broader Catholic tradition, specifically through Catholic social teachings, which define Catholic identity as communal and social in nature. The Catholic Social Tradition is a wonderful branch of Catholic teachings, faith and life that very few Catholics know about. Its focus is social justice, and its foundation is a communal sense of the human grounded in the inner-Trinitarian, communal life of God.

The communal and social sense of identity in both Latina spirituality and Catholic social teachings does not accept community in an uncritical fashion. Instead, it envisions an egalitarian community where injustice is condemned and a true sense of communion is embraced. The element of justice will therefore appear as a central theme within Latina spirituality. Our spirituality is not a detached, otherworldly experience of the sacred. Rather, Latina spirituality is rooted in the everyday lives and rituals of the Latina community. Spirituality is not something that is understood as isolated from the rest of our lives; it saturates our lives. Latinas' sense of family and community is broad, including the extended family, the saints and the dead. Latina community becomes a sacred space where the dead, the saintly and the living come together. Latina understandings of community also celebrate the diversity that is the Latina population. You find this in the appearances of non-Christian elements within our spirituality. These spaces where non-Christian elements enter into our spiritual lives bear witness to the indigenous and African presence in Latin American and Latina cultures and histories. This can be a site of struggle and tension for us, as later sections of this book will discuss.

Latinas represent a group that cannot be reduced to one race; thus, Latina spirituality does not understand diversity as a hindrance but instead as a pathway to the divine. Categorizing groups under one racial-ethnic heading can be helpful, but it often glosses over the diversity and differences within our communities. Too often in the United States, diversity is seen as divisive. But for Latinas, diversity is celebrated because we recognize our unity within, not in spite of, our diversity. This concern for respecting and affirming diversity within unity is a key issue plaguing the current political global climate. We live in a world where two simultaneous and often contradictory trends coexist: globalization and what is often called tribalism. Globalization refers to the growing interconnectedness of the world via technology, communications and commerce. While there are many positive factors linked to globalization—notably a stronger sense of the global human community as a whole—there are also negative effects. One such negative effect is the growing homogenization of the world, especially in the spread of American popular culture throughout the globe. With the spread of McDonald's, Starbucks and shows like *Grey's Anatomy,* the world's diversity is leveled. Local cultures are threatened by the sameness of U.S. culture and its dominance in other countries and societies. One way to protest the relentless march of U.S. culture across the world is tribalism, or a strong affirmation of one's local identity. Communities strongly emphasize their local identity in response to what they see as the threat of globalized culture. In Latin America this is seen in the growth of pan-indigenous movements in countries like Guatemala and Bolivia which focus on the traditional culture and identity of native peoples and affirm a return to native dress and customs.

Within the U.S. landscape this homogenization is clearly seen in the call for immigrants to assimilate to the dominant U.S. ethos.

Indeed, Latinas, who often maintain the Spanish language and close ties to their local communities, are often seen as a group that is not willing to "jump on board" and fully adapt to U.S. culture. Our desire to treasure our heritage is seen as our downfall and a threat to unity in the U.S. However, Latina spirituality affirms that this celebration of our particular culture is in fact an entry point into true unity. I often tell my students that one cannot be passionate about abstract concepts such as justice and liberation. You cannot rally around a term. Instead, it is through the individual stories of social-justice and liberation struggles that one becomes impassioned for a cause. It is through the very particular that we tap into the broader human experience. This is why autobiography and narrative are such powerful writing styles that speak to us. Therefore, for us to enter into the world of Latina spirituality we must first pause and describe this community in its diversity and unity. It is also through the particular flavor of Latinas that the broader connections are made with other racial and ethnic groups.

CHAPTER ONE

• A LATINA UNDERSTANDING OF COMMUNITY AND SELF •

Claudia came to the United States to be a nanny. At least that was what the "coyote" told her family when he took their two thousand dollars and promised them to "take care of their girl." After what seemed like weeks in the back of a van cramped with other young Central American girls, Claudia emerged squinting in the humid Florida sun. They were not in Miami, as she was promised, but on what seemed like a farm. She learned, much to her and her traveling partners' despair, that they would not be nannies but instead prostitutes in a brothel for the work camp. They would have to sleep with strange men to pay off their families' debts. After weeks in the brothel Claudia feels trapped and dirty. The brothel is heavily guarded, and even if she could escape, what would she do? Go to U.S. authorities and be deported? Bring shame upon her family? There is a woman, she is told, who is trying to help them. She says they do have rights. Claudia is afraid. She also does not know if she can trust the woman, who is Salvadoran like herself. After all, wasn't the coyote that betrayed her and her family Salvadoran too?

The Latina Community

Latinas constitute the largest "minority" population in the United States. This is a dubious classification, for the U.S. census data on which it is based collapses racial categories (such as African American or Black) and ethno-cultural categories (such as Hispanic and Asian American) under one heading. While this community is diverse in terms of race, country of origin and culture, there are certain features communities classified as Latina share: a history of Spanish colonialism, the Spanish language (whether spoken or not) and a Catholic heritage. I realize that bilingualism is not a reality for every Latina. We cannot assume that all Latinas in the U.S. speak Spanish. At the same time, Latinas are distinguished by their linguistic heritage. While uniting a community under the banner of Spanish colonialism may seem odd in the twenty-first century, Spanish culture has indeed left an indelible imprint on Latin American and Latina cultures. The most notable of these is the influence of Roman Catholic culture on Latina culture. While not every Latina is Roman Catholic, the Roman Catholic stamp on all Latina culture, regardless of one's religious affiliation, is a clear legacy of Spanish colonialism. This shared legacy, however, must be situated within the diversity of Latin American communities. The added factor of living in the U.S. further complicates their sense of identity.

Latinas struggle with the question of identity on a daily basis. They often describe themselves as bridge people whose lives "on the hyphen" mean that they are never fully comfortable in the two contexts we straddle. On one side you find the country of your heritage, whether you were born in Latin America or your parents are from there. Often this Latin American culture is a key feature within our identity. On the other side is the United States. These two worlds meet in us, and we often feel that we do not fully belong to either. Therefore we are part of those two worlds, yet those worlds never fully accept us. We are too "Latina" for the dominant U.S. ethos, yet at the same time we are too "gringo" for Latin Americans. Thus we find recurring themes in Latina scholarship of exile, mixture and the border. Some Latinas, in particular some Cuban Americans, identify themselves as exiles living away from their homelands. For either political or economic reasons they live away from their home countries. Yet they maintain a strong sense of connection with their native communities. There are also those Latinas who did not come to the U.S., but instead had the U.S. forced upon them. Both the Puerto Rican and Mexican American experiences share this reality. The Puerto Rican experience is one of U.S. colonialism which resulted in migration to the mainland. The 1903 Platt Amendment ended what we in the U.S. call the Spanish-American war, which was in fact Cuba and Puerto Rico's wars of independence from Spain. This Amendment made Puerto Rico a U.S. colony and gave the U.S. the right to intervene as it saw fit in Cuba's foreign and domestic policies. Puerto Ricans' status as second-class U.S. citizens makes their sense of identity and sense of worth extremely problematic. Mexican-Americans often joke that many of them did not cross the border, but in fact, the border crossed them. This refers to the historical acquisition of former Mexican lands by the U.S. government through the 1848 Treaty of Guadalupe Hidalgo. One day, many Mexicans awoke to find themselves living in the United States even though they had not budged an inch.

Not surprisingly, the Latin American or Spanish stamp on the United States remains, even though U.S. dominant culture tries to write it out of its history. Scholars study the former British colonies but do not study St. Augustine as the first true European colony in what is today known as the United States. The U.S. remains marked by this history, seen in the very names of our cities and states. Cities such as Santa Monica, San Jose and Los Angeles remind us of the Spanish (and Catholic) heritage of these lands. States such as Montana (mountain in Spanish), Colorado (*colored* in Spanish), and New Mexico still bear traces of the Spanish colonial history. It should not surprise us that over half of the Latina population in the U.S. lives in the Southwest. And yet, the Latina reality is in a constant state of flux. While some Latinas are U.S. citizens, acceptance within mainstream U.S. society is difficult because of the radical differences between Hispanic and U.S. cultures. Two factors that most distinguish U.S. from Hispanic culture are the secularism and individualism which permeates U.S. ideology.

Individualism and Secularism

Unlike the secularism which pervades U.S. society, Latina culture cannot be separated from its Catholic heritage. The Spanish colonialization of Latin America created a distinct culture unlike that of the mostly Protestant United States. This is a vital distinction. Asserting the Roman Catholic heritage of the Latina people is not the same as claiming that all Latinas are Roman Catholic. Rather, I intend to lift up the intrinsic Catholicism of the Hispanic community. The United States is often cited as a secular country, and it is in fact secularism that is often at the heart of many radical religious critiques of U.S. culture as a whole. This may seem paradoxical for some of us in the United States, where we have recently had a confessed evangelical president who counts pastors among his top advisors, where our money says "In God we trust" and the Pledge of Allegiance states that the U.S. is "one nation under God." It is also difficult to understand the U.S. as secular when we look at the current prominence of conservative-minded Christians in politics. Nonetheless, we do maintain distinctions between church and state, and we are not a theocratic nation. While many argue that the dominant U.S. culture is Christian in nature, it is not Christian on paper.

Nonetheless, the more secular nature of the United States in relation to Latin American countries becomes visible when we look at the growing secularism of Latinas living in this country compared to the very central role of religious life in their home countries. While much has been made of the exodus of Roman Catholic Latinas to Protestant denominations, most notably Pentecostalism, what is becoming even more significant is the departure of Latinas from churches as a whole. Surveys reveal that more and more Latinas are becoming more secular as they assimilate into U.S. culture. This change is seen concretely in their lack of church attendance. Recent immigrants who report regular church attendance in their home countries now participate less and less. Several factors are cited, the most notable being the contrast between Latin American countries which are heavily marked by ecclesial calendars (i.e. saints' days, feast days) and the more secular calendar of the United States. Many Latinas cite the busyness of U.S. life as another contributing factor. For Latinas who work full time, the weekend is the only time to catch up on chores and do housework. These Latinas still identify as Catholic, yet they are less and less institutionally affiliated.

For two years I lived in a Mayan town in the highlands of Guatemala. This was perhaps the most profound experience in my life. I spent two years working with a Roman Catholic mission that does social justice work with the local indigenous community. There were many dimensions of my time in Guatemala that marked it as radically distinct from my time in the U.S.: the rural location, the conditions of poverty, the lack of water and, at times, electricity. However, one of the clearest markers of my time in Guatemala was the way life revolved around the Roman Catholic liturgical calendar. Life was marked by patron saint festivals, Corpus Christi, processions in the streets. You went to church at night for meetings and prayer groups because frankly, there wasn't much else to do otherwise. The church played a central role in the rhythm of the community. That is something I miss now that I have returned to the United States, where, though I teach in a religious studies department, I had class on Good Friday, an anathema to most Latin American Catholics.

Linked to the secularism of U.S. culture is its overarching individualism. The individualism of U.S. society is alien to the collective consciousness of Latina culture. While the U.S. is a "me" society, Latina culture is a "we" society. The individualistic, competitive nature of U.S. society creates an environment in which the family-oriented and communal nature of Latina culture is utterly foreign. As a consequence, U.S. Hispanics are perceived as lazy, backward underachievers who do not possess the edge to make it in the U.S. For the Hispanic, success is not necessarily measured by individual accomplishments. In the U.S. the individual is primary. We see this in the emphasis on individual rights, responsibilities, and liberties. The communal nature of Latina culture in the U.S. is constantly being called into question and misunderstood. Whether it is the Latina tendency to have extended families living together (albeit sometimes due to poverty) or their strong sense of obligation toward their families, the "I" in Latina culture always has a "we" behind it, in spite of the dominant U.S. culture of assimilation. As we will see in the later sections about Marian Latina devotions, this emphasis on community and a sense of the divine speaking through and to the rejected ones, is fundamental in Latina spirituality.

Latina Theology

A key source for understanding Latina spirituality is the work of Latina theologians in the United States. Latina theologians are a diverse group of Latinas representing various Latin American nations and sociopolitical commitments. They draw from the cultural sources of everyday Latina spirituality as a starting point and central feature of their work. Therefore, as I write this text I do not write alone, and I must recognize the contributions that other Latinas have made to the study of Latina spirituality. Similar to the framing of Latina spirituality, Latina theology represents a group of women working together to give voice to their communities. The women I cite in these next few paragraphs, and throughout this text, are not only academic colleagues but friends and fellow sisters in the struggle. Not all Latina theologians represent a feminist interpretation of Latina experiences, though many are influenced by feminist scholarship within theology. Some, like Ana María Pineda, embrace an emphasis on Latina culture without employing feminist theory or categories. Others, like myself, see the egalitarian vision of the sexes at the heart of feminism as key to our study of women's spirituality.

Gloria Loya's work articulates a Hispanic feminist approach that investigates vital expressions of Hispanic faith and culture as a theological resource. Loya offers three sources that inform her Hispanic feminist methodology. Narration, specifically the voice of community leader Dolores Huerta, is a first font. Her second source is more analytical: an examination of two Mexican legendry female figures: the image of Malintzín and Our Lady of Guadalupe. A third resource is the writings of seventeenth-century thinker Sor Juana Inés de la Cruz. Loya's work highlights various important themes within Latina spirituality. The importance of social justice struggles is found through her emphasis on Dolores Huerta's narrative voice as a co-founder of the United Farm Workers' Movement. Huerta becomes a model of the activist Latina who was deeply informed by her faith. Malantzín is the legendary concubine of Hernando Cortés, the great conqueror of the Aztec empire. Malantzín, as Cortés' indigenous translator and eventual lover, is seen by the Mexican people as the great betrayer of her people. On the other extreme is Our Lady of Guadalupe, the most revered symbol of womanhood in Mexican culture. Loya notes that Latinas are often judged by these two extremes: the ideal virgin or the betrayer whore. This creates a limited construction of Latinas' sexuality and identity. You are either a pure, good girl who rejects her sexuality as evil or a bad girl who allows her lusts and passions to define her life. Finally, in highlighting the work of poet, dramatist and theologian Sor Juana Inés de la Cruz, Loya emphasizes the intellectual contribution Latin American women make. This is vital for us, for our intellectual foremothers are often written out of the canons of academic history.

In a similar vein Jeanette Rodríguez's scholarship emphasizes Our Lady of Guadalupe as a source of empowerment for Mexican-American women and the importance of oral tradition and cultural memory for Latina spirituality. This is why the Latinas' everyday faith is fundamental within Latina theology. The stories of our mothers and grandmothers are not found in the great theological treatises studied in universities and seminaries. They are instead remembered and lived in our spiritual lives. This is also why Latina scholars include the voices of everyday grassroots Latinas. Their stories and struggles are cited along with the other greats of the Christian theological tradition. The most common way that these voices are captured is through the use of ethnography: a process of interviewing Latinas and drawing theological insights from their concrete voices and experiences. In my own research on Mayan women, I have found their stories of faith amidst the terrifying years of the thirty-six-year civil war in Guatemala to be a challenging source for my own theology. They describe kidnapped family members, rape and their own children killed before their eyes. Yet in the same breath, they speak of the forgiveness and compassion that is central to their Christian spirituality. Their stories and faith describe forgiveness in ways that academics cannot. This forgiveness is key to Jesus' gospel message and to the teaching of loving our enemies. However, academic Latina scholars like myself see their stories as fundamental to our theology.

Latina feminist theology is a liberation theology with a multi-layered analysis of U.S. Latina existence. Latina feminist theology reflects on the divine emerging from the context of a marginalized people. Liberation theologies represent a group of theological movements that exploded onto the academic and pastoral scene in the 1960s. They placed the non-person, the oppressed, marginalized masses, at the center and starting point of theological reflection. Often they are described as approaching Christianity "from the underside of history," highlighting the silenced voices in historical and contemporary churches. Liberation theologians also highlight the ways in which Christianity has been used as a tool of oppression and how this distorts the authentic Christian message of liberation. The two most well-known of these movements, and the ones that also happen to be most influential on Latina theology, are Latin American and feminist theologies.

Latin American liberation theology is both a grassroots pastoral and academic movement. Latin American liberation theology places the poor at the center of Christian reflection. Relying heavily on gospel teachings, Latin American liberation theologians claim that central to Christian life is authentic active solidarity with poor people. When I first arrived in Guatemala and began interviewing men and women about the impact the Roman Catholic mission had upon their lives, one answer was repeatedly expressed. Before the clinic and the school, before the fair trade coffee and the new houses, the priests' message of their creation in the image of God is what truly liberated and empowered them. For a Mayan people—who had been told for decades that they were nothing, without value—to hear that they too were God's children was the foundation of all the concrete social justice work that was to come in the future.

Feminist theologians examine the sexism that has tainted classic Christian constructions of male and female identity as well as the unjust, concrete ecclesial practices that emerged from these stereotypes. Feminist theologians argue that this hierarchical, patriarchal understanding of humanity is contrary to the authentic Christian message. While the sources of Latina feminist theology cannot be reduced to these two theological movements, it is from these theologies that Latina feminist theologians derive their analysis of the economic, patriarchal and ethnocentric structures and constructs that oppress Latinas.

Latina feminist theologians often work on related topics, but they are not a homogeneous, self-proclaimed group of scholars. Their commonalties include feminist critical analysis, contextual accent and a liberationist emphasis in their work. Informed by these analyses, these theologians destabilize androcentric and hierarchical theologies, offering an emancipatory vision that promotes the full humanity of all. Within Latina feminist theology, some call themselves Latina feminists while others embrace the term *mujerista*. *Mujerista* theology is a voice within Latina feminist liberation theology that privileges the voices and grassroots struggles of Latinas. It is primarily articulated by Ada María Isasi-Díaz. *Mujerista* theology emphasizes a multi-faceted analysis of Latinas' lives and contexts, including how gender, race, ethnicity and class shape Latina identity in the United States. Its methodology is marked by its use of ethnography and the inclusion of grassroots Latina voices within academic theology and pastoral movements. By taking the time and energy to interview grassroots Latinas and incorporating their voice and insights in academic work, *mujerista* theology affirms their intellectual contributions.

Mestizaje and *Mulatez*

The *mestizaje/mulatez* of the Hispanic people is yet another ambiguity of the Hispanic reality. *Mestizaje* refers to the biological and cultural mixing of indigenous and Spanish cultures that occurred as a result of the conquest of the Americas; *mulatez* refers to the mixture of Spanish and African cultures that occurred as a result of the transatlantic slave trade. Contrary to popular belief, Latinas are not a single race. They are a combination of various races which cover the entire color spectrum of humanity. This mixture makes it difficult to reduce Latinas to the current racial paradigms of the United States. It does not help either that the United States often operates under a black-and-white binary concerning race in which you are either one or the other. Based on their inability to fit into that black/white model of racism, Latinas are often either glossed over as people of color or entirely ignored in racial discussions. Latinas are not a monolithic group. In fact, until recently, Latinas did not embrace a collective identification of themselves (and in many ways, they still do not) but instead identified themselves by their countries of origin. However, the term Latina is an accepted political construction that we embrace in order to promote unity in our communities when we struggle against social and ethnic discrimination. For example, when people ask me quite bluntly, "What are you?" I always answer "Cuban-American." I never answer "Latina." At the same time, I am well aware that the term *Latina* is a helpful way to connect myself to the struggles and concerns of a wider community that shares many of the same issues I encounter in terms of identity, culture and spirituality.

A Latina Understanding of What it Means to be Human

Within Latina theological scholarship, the work of Ada María Isasi-

Díaz has the clearest articulation of a theological anthropology that highlights the Latina communal sensibility. Theological anthropology is the area in theological scholarship that examines what it means to be human, created in the image of God. This understanding of the human addresses not only our relationship with our divine creator but also how that relationship influences and shapes our relationship with our fellow and sister human beings and vice versa. In her essay "Elements of a *Mujerista* Anthropology," Isasi-Díaz holds three phrases as critical to elaborating her *mujerista* anthropology: *la lucha* (the struggle), *permítanme hablar* (allow me to speak) and *la comunidad/la familia* (community / family).[1] These elements are not exclusive to Latinas, but embody a sense of our humanity that goes well beyond Latina culture. These phrases become the starting point for reflection: Latinas' daily lives (*lo cotidiano*), their contributive voices and their relational conception of selfhood. The term *lo cotidiano* (daily life) saturates the work of both Latinos and Latinas as they describe their spirituality. It is a term that appears repeatedly throughout this text. Claiming *lo cotidiano* as a source for spirituality has a significant impact on the manner in which we understand our vital sources of knowledge and love of God. Often we think that the voices of the academically educated are the most privileged sources for our intellectual formulations. However, in claiming *lo cotidiano*, Latinas embrace everyday life as a source of knowledge and spirituality.

The first element, struggle (*la lucha*), is a fundamental category for Latina understandings of the human because it recognizes the trials and tribulations that are part of life. We do not want to reduce our lives to struggles against injustice, but we do want to highlight the truth that life is a struggle, that things do not come easily and that this struggle deeply infuses our spirituality. This is clearly seen in the importance given to the crucified Jesus in Latina spirituality. The suffering Jesus of Good Friday is significant to Latinas because it shows us that God understands and accompanies us in our struggles and suffering. I will return to this point a bit later when we look at Good Friday devotions more closely. However, this emphasis on *la lucha* is not, I would argue, exclusive to Latina spirituality. Many women find moments of spiritual depth in their deepest trials and tribulations. Our daily struggles mark all of our lives. Too often, spirituality focuses on the detached and the other-worldly. To emphasize the struggle is to encounter God in the concreteness of this world. Isasi-Díaz highlights the concreteness of the struggle and its implications for spirituality when she discusses the importance of the picket line and the spirituality of protest. Reacting against an otherworldy, highly ritualized, individualistic and compartmentalized understanding of spirituality, Isasi-Díaz describes involvement in the struggle against injustice as an active form of spirituality. She discusses her social-justice work as a concrete expression of her communal spirituality. To protest on behalf of workers' rights is a spiritual act. Social action is a form of prayer. To decry injustice is to protest those social structures that deny the full humanity of all of God's creation and is ultimately to do God's work here on earth.

A second important category is *permítanme hablar*, translated as "allow me to speak." This dimension of our humanity recognizes the need for Latinas, and in fact all women, to have a voice and authority in their lives. For Roman Catholic laywomen this is especially important, for the institutional church does not offer many avenues for our authoritative voices within the hierarchy. Our work is often found at the grassroots level, for example through religious education. We are not considered privileged sources of knowledge and spirituality. To allow us to speak is to affirm our contribution to Catholic spirituality. To allow us to speak is to take into consideration our particular insights and concerns. I find this category of particular importance to young women because so often their voices are too easily dismissed. While there is definitely a certain wisdom that comes with age and experience, this does not mean that young women do not have a powerful voice within spirituality. I am constantly amazed and challenged by the contributions of my undergraduate students who push me to look at the world through their eyes. The particular challenges they face and the impact their spiritual lives have upon them broaden my understanding of spirituality. I have been especially moved by the spirit of volunteerism I find in so many young adults who are living out their faith through service. To allow them to speak is to offer a more inclusive vision of women's spirituality. The importance of family and community—Isasi-Díaz's final category—is one we have already discussed in light of Latina culture. However, I would like to connect it more broadly to Roman Catholic spirituality as a whole.

Catholic Social Teaching

The communal nature of the self embraced by Latina culture is not foreign to, but is in fact embedded in, a Roman Catholic worldview that promotes a communal understanding of the human. This is seen strongly in the Catholic social tradition, also described as Catholic social teaching. A primary emphasis of these social teachings is the intersection of faith and everyday life. Its method is characterized by three moments: "see, judge and act." They counsel us to assess, theologically judge and then respond to the struggles and concerns of the world around us. Two concrete examples are offered. On the more institutional or hierarchical level of the church, Catholic social teachings are found in official documents written by bishops or the pope. These documents address a particular social issue and offer theological reflection in light of Catholic teachings. They also include a call for action. The birth of this tradition is firmly situated in the 1891 papal encyclical *Rerum Novarum*, which dealt with the question of workers' rights. If you read this document, you find a Catholic call for a fair wage for workers and an affirmation of their rights. The document "sees" the late nineteenth century context of industrialization, urbanization and poverty; "judges" the mistreatment and unjust conditions of workers in light of their full humanity as God's creation; and calls for the "acts" of workers' rights.

This "see-judge-act" model is one you can apply to your daily spirituality. This model is informed and remembered by attentiveness to the world around us and its connection to our relationship with the divine. A wonderful example is found in Jim Keady's advocacy for sweatshop workers. When Jim was a graduate student at St. John's University, he was assigned a research paper on the Catholic social tradition. He also coached the soccer team, which was at the time negotiating an endorsement deal with Nike, which meant that all of their athletes and coaches would wear Nike apparel. Jim decided to research Nike to see if the company met the standards of Catholic teachings in terms of dignity of the human person. Given their gross labor abuses particularly in Asia, Nike failed miserably. Keady challenged his university. He felt that a Catholic university should embody the principles of Catholicism. The university told him to wear Nike or resign from the team. Jim resigned, moved to Indonesia and actually tried to work in one of Nike's factories. Nike, however, would not allow this, so Jim tried to replicate the living conditions of some of those workers and lived that way himself, hoping to get a firsthand sense of the lives of these exploited people. He is now completing a documentary on his experiences (www.sweatthefilm.org). His advocacy is an inspiring example of this see-judge-act model. While not all of us have to move to Indonesia, there are ways we can embody this spirit in our daily lives by being attentive to the clothing we buy, the coffee we drink, and educated about whether or not the companies we support promote unjust and therefore un-Catholic labor practices. For me, intentionally drinking and buying fair trade coffee is a spiritual act of solidarity with the millions of coffee pickers around the globe.

A central dimension of the Catholic social tradition is the notion of the common good. The common good emphasizes group and communal fulfillment over individualism. The foundation of the common good is an understanding of the human as made in God's Triune image (*imago Dei*). The Christian belief in humanity's creation in the image of

God is foundational to understanding who we are. The book of Genesis opens with two creation stories, accounts that have captured theological and popular imagination for centuries. Whether it is the writings of the earliest Christian thinkers, contemporary debates on intelligent design versus evolution or a *Simpsons* cartoon's humorous reinterpretation of Adam and Eve, no other section of the Hebrew Scriptures has provoked as much creativity and debate as the first three chapters of Genesis. Belief in the image of God within humanity is grounded in the first of these creation stories. The pivotal line is found in chapter one, verse 27: "So God created humankind in his image, in the image of God he created them; male and female he created them." This statement has been a central point of contention and a foundation for Christian understandings of men and women for centuries. The notion that humanity is created in the image of God, distinguishing us from the rest of creation, and the exact meaning of that image, continues to produce awe and challenge the religious imagination of Christians.

Our Relational Humanity

The image in which we are created is a relational Trinity that exists in community. Thus the image of God in us represents the communal dimension of humanity. Christians believe that God is monotheistic yet at the same time Triune. God exists as Creator, Sustainer and Redeemer, as a community of three in one. Therefore, the image of God within us must be communal and social. We must understand our salvation as social. Our lives are intimately connected to the rest of humanity. This is very different from the U.S. individualism discussed above. Within Catholic social teachings, the common good highlights this communal model of humanity and more importantly, our essential self-understanding. Harmony, order, balance and solidarity mark the common good. The communion that is humanity mirrors the communion of the Trinity that must be enacted through solidarity.

Having been born and raised in the United States in a Cuban family that strongly emphasized Cuban cultural roots and practices, there are certain things about the U.S. that still jar me. One of the most frequent is the manner in which we in the States usually introduce ourselves. Upon meeting someone, usually the first (if not second or third question) that is posed to me is "What do you do?" In other words, it is my job or profession that defines me. This is very different from the Latina mindset. Latinas ask where you are from, where your family is from and may even try to see if they know one of your relatives. It is the relationship with your community, not your job, that is important. This communal understanding of humanity that is theologically understood as Trinitarian is at the center of Catholic theology and has been strongly emphasized by feminist theologians. A feminist Trinitarian understanding of the *imago Dei* places relationships at the center. It is through our relationships that we most concretely reflect God's image. This Trinitarian notion of the image of God also gives us a theological grounding for our relationships with each other. Relationality becomes the essence of God's image and our human nature. The mutual relational love of the Trinity as expressed through the concrete life and ministry of Jesus becomes the foundation for an egalitarian understanding of our relationships and their formalizations within community. The Latina sense of community is not naïve, for it highlights the ambiguity and oppression found within Latina communities. This focus adds a critical edge to Catholic understandings of community, in which the dynamics of power are not always at the forefront. The Latina vision of community and family is one where justice reigns. It is an egalitarian model, based on an egalitarian vision of the human.

Finding Meaning in Everyday Life

As important as home and family are, the lives of Latinas cannot be reduced to the private realm. In general, public space is seen as the realm of the male while private space is seen as an exclusively feminine domain. This is even the case in families with children where both parents hold jobs. Too often, the burdens of parenting are placed exclusively on mothers; fathers' contributions are seen as "helping out."

Ultimately, the private realm is devalued in comparison with the public realm. The feminist mantra "The personal is political," is one way of approaching this Latina insight. In claiming that the personal is in fact politically significant, feminists are claiming that the personal has value and affects society. Latina emphasis on everyday life and its theological value becomes a way of politicizing the personal. The relationships we model in our homes are the foundation of our societal relationships. If you are raised in a household in which women are disrespected and have little authority, you are likely to be wary of women in authority in work and politics. To emphasize the value of everyday life is to highlight that our sources of knowledge need to be expanded from the private, abstract and academic if we truly want to include marginalized voices. This is part of Latinas' historical legacy. In my own work on historical Latina theology and spirituality, I was delighted to find in the writings of Sor Juana Inés de la Cruz an emphasis on everyday life as a source for knowledge.

Sor Juana Inés de la Cruz was a seventeenth century nun, considered the most significant voice in Latin American colonial letters. Many scholars also see her as the first feminist of the Americas. Sor Juana's extensive corpus consists of poetry, drama, devotional writings and prose. These writings are heavily marked by theological and philosophical themes and sources. It is her interest in these areas that eventually led to the tragic final years of her life. Sor Juana spent the majority of her life as a cloistered nun, yet, in spite of this, became an internationally recognized scholar during her lifetime. She struggled with her decision to enter religious life, yet because she had a strong aversion to marriage, she took the veil. In colonial Mexico, the only alternatives for women of a certain social class were marriage or convent life. Sor Juana chose the latter. Part of the reason she favored convent life was her passion for reading and writing. She felt the convent would be a more appropriate space to pursue her passions.

Both the court and the church commissioned Sor Juana to write poetry and plays. Her fame began to draw the negative attention of the ecclesial hierarchy, who felt a cloistered nun should not be recognized for her brilliant writings. Ironically, it is not her popular secular poetry and plays that eventually led to her silencing, but her choice to venture into the male-dominated field of theology. While the details of the final years of her life remain murky, it is clear that she renounced writing and took a vow of silence in the final years of her life, due in large part to ecclesial pressure in response to her theological critique of a Jesuit's sermon. Sor Juana dared to write in the one area that was forbidden to women; she dared to assume that women could have something meaningful and intellectual to say about the divine.

One of Sor Juana's last writings is *La Respuesta a Sor Filotea* (*The Response*), her autobiographical justification for women's right to education. Weaving Scripture, theology, philosophy and litanies of mythological, biblical and historical women who preceded her, Sor Juana argues that her intellect is a gift from God and not a curse. This piece is considered by many to be the first feminist theological writing in the Americas. In one section of *The Response*, Sor Juana tells us of a time when the Inquisition forbade her from reading for three months. She does not explain why this occurred but blames the prohibition on the initiative of her mother superior. Most likely, however, it was the nature of her reading that caught the attention of church authorities. Non-Christian philosophers such as Plato and Aristotle were considered inappropriate for anyone to read, especially a cloistered nun, yet it is clear from her writings that Sor Juana had access to these books. While preventing her from studying texts, the prohibition was not capable of ensnaring Sor Juana's mind. Instead of studying books, she studied the world around her. For Sor Juana, all of God's creation was a suitable object of study, down to the minutest creature, for it revealed God's greatness and glory.

What, then, did Sor Juana study? She observed the world around her within the convent. She studied daily life. Her study of the architecture of the dormitories led to lessons on geometry. Noting that visual perspective does not always produce a geometrically accurate depiction of the planes where walls and ceiling meet, Sor Juana wondered if these "delusions of the eye" led to the incorrect assumption that the world was flat. The pleasure of watching two girls playing top was interrupted by "this madness of mine," and Sor Juana turned the exercise into a scientific experiment with flour to discern whether the top moved in circles or spirals. This led to experiments in the kitchen. She found that cooking with eggs led to a wealth of knowledge. On these culinary experiments she writes, "What can we women know, save philosophies of the kitchen?" Sor Juana is sarcastically challenging the caricature that the activities that are gender-coded as women's are somehow thoughtless and lacking in intellectual valor. This comment is closely followed by perhaps the most delightful statement in Sor Juana's corpus, "Had Aristotle cooked, he would have written a great deal more."[2]

Common experience becomes the source of philosophical reflection. Through her experimentation, Sor Juana explored alternative sources for knowledge, especially in the sphere traditionally attributed to women. By equating the knowledge acquired in the private women's sphere to that of the great philosophers and theologians she read extensively, Sor Juana constitutes the woman's private arena as a space for rational reflection. Centuries before the category appeared in the writings of modern feminists, Sor Juana demonstrated the significance of daily life for transforming the very nature of our spiritual and intellectual sources.

These theologies and philosophies "of the kitchen" are the center of Latina spirituality. We will not find Latinas' stories in the great theological treatises of Christian history or the official ecclesial documents of the church. Instead, we find them in their devotions, everyday spirituality and lived religious experiences. Sor Juana reminds us that Latinas' struggle for access to education and a public voice is one that has deep historical roots. She offers one avenue for correcting this exclusion. Within the Christian tradition, examples like Sor Juana do not stand alone. Scripture stories such as the account of the Hebrew midwives in the Exodus narrative also serve as biblical sources for a Latina spirituality. Much like Shiphrah and Puah, whose refusal to obey the pharaoh's order to kill Hebrew sons became a pivotal moment in the Exodus narrative (Exodus 1:15–21), so too Latinas contribute to their communities often behind the scenes. We know Moses' name, yet many do not know Shiphrah and Puah's, despite the fact that without them the liberation of the Hebrew people would never have occurred. Similarly, we often do not know the names of Latinas who have contributed to Catholic spirituality and community. This book places Latina spirituality at its center, examining how particular Latina devotions inform a Catholic spirituality that places community and communion at its center. Through an examination of Latina Marian devotions, popular religion and the centrality of the crucified Jesus, I will explore this particular Catholic spirituality that speaks to those well beyond ethnic or racial lines.

FOOD FOR THOUGHT

1. What is your racial, ethnic and cultural background? How does mixture play a role in it? How do you feel about this "mix"? How does it affect your spirituality?

2. How is Catholic identity distinct from the dominant U.S. culture's individualism?

3. Does your cultural background emphasize family and community or individualism? How does this emphasis shape your spirituality?

4. What are some images that evoke the image of God in humanity? What does it mean to understand that image as Trinitarian and relational?

PRAYER FOR COMMUNITY

Invocation:
Loving Spirit, guide us.
Wise Spirit, teach us.
Just Spirit, empower us.

Scripture: The Hebrew Midwives: Exodus 1:15-21

Response: Let us pray for God's loving Spirit to guide us when we face difficult challenges.
Loving Spirit, embrace us.
Let us pray for God's wise Spirit to teach us to accept and celebrate ourselves and our diversity.
Loving Spirit, educate us.
Let us pray for God's just Spirit to empower us in the face of injustice.
Just Spirit, feed us.

CHAPTER TWO

• THE AMERICAN CHURCH •

"Byron Manuel has evil eye." My mother-in-law said this to me ominously,
studying my face intently for my reaction. I shrugged and answered, "So
rub an egg over him." This was my standard response to her spiritual
assessments of my son's health. It was also not what I was truly thinking. What I was thinking was that he was eleven months old and
teething. However, I had learned that such responses were not welcome
in the Guatemalan community where I had been living for the past two
years. Most afflictions, even ones that had medical explanations, also
had spiritual causes.

By now I was an old pro at evil eye. My husband was diagnosed
one day by his mother. His stomach had been bugging him and he was
listless. I suspected parasites, something that I had become quite familiar with since I moved to Guatemala. My diagnosis was rejected. She
rubbed an egg on him, chanting Catholic prayers and making the sign
of the cross over his body. This egg was then broken in a glass of water
and placed under our bed overnight as he slept. The yolk revealed in the
morning that it was indeed evil eye. Another egg was rubbed over him
and he was "cured." The next day he woke up with a fever, vomiting. I
sent a sample to the lab, purchased antibiotics and smugly informed my
mother-in-law that he indeed had parasites. My diagnosis and my
smugness were not well received.

I am perhaps giving a bit too antagonistic of an impression. I get
along fabulously with my mother-in-law and for the most part welcome her religious beliefs (what many scholars would call superstitions

or folk religion) into our lives. I avoided dogs having sex and drunk men on the streets (a frequent sight in a poor town like San Lucas) when I was pregnant and when my son was an infant, for they were sure bearers of evil eye. I usually remembered to tie the red ribbon with a scabbard on it around Byron Manuel's wrist when we left the house, knowing that if I didn't I would be chastised by all the women in my new family. When I came home and found my mother-in-law or my husband's aunts looking at me with a tinge of guilt, I did not reprimand them for the inevitable egg I would find under my son's crib. However, they could sense that in spite of the fact that I was Cuban-American and a scholar of religion, I did not take them 100 percent seriously.

Back to my son's evil eye. This evil eye is different, I am informed. My mother-in-law does not have the power to heal it. I must take Byron Manuel to a spiritual healer for three consecutive days to cure him. Upon hearing this, my husband tells me to go. He says that it is out of respect for his mother. However, I can tell he is worried. There are tales floating around town of children who died from evil eye, whose parents did not treat the affliction. Their mothers' skepticism killed them. I can tell my husband is wondering if my skepticism will harm our son. So I go. I am a good Cuban girl who has been raised to respect her elders and, frankly, the religious scholar in me wants to see what is going to happen. An old woman rubs my son with herbs making the sign of the cross repeatedly over every inch of Byron Manuel's body. He does not writhe in agony as the curse is removed. In fact, it tickles him. This satchel of herbs is thrown in the fire and crackles loudly, signaling the presence of evil eye. The same ritual is repeated each day, and by the third day, I must admit, the crackling is much weaker.

Did my son have evil eye? I don't know. He did not seem any different to me after this ritual, but everyone is relieved and much more relaxed once it is completed. The threat of evil eye has been lifted from our family. I am not sure if it is the *curandera* (faith or spiritual healer) or the tube of Baby Orajel that a friend brings me from the States that cures him. I do know that this is a ritual purification that is important for the community where I am living, my second home, and that I must respect it. Evil eye is a widespread belief in this community, and its origins date back to Spanish folk religion. Children are most susceptible to evil eye, especially infants, which is why the custom in Guatemala is that neither a newborn nor his mother should leave their home until forty days after childbirth. What are described as "hot" forces give evil eye, which is why drunk men and menstruating and pregnant women must be avoided, for one can transmit evil eye without knowing it. One can also intentionally give evil eye, and this is usually due to envy. The symptoms of evil eye include vomiting, listlessness, irritability and waking up suddenly throughout the night.

Anthropologist Sheila Cosminsky has noted that one of the effects of the understanding of evil eye in Guatemala is that women's social roles become more limited. Indeed, the burden of protecting one's child falls exclusively on the mother. Cosminsky also points out that evil is used to explain the innocent suffering of children. Since most cases of evil eye are accidental, the giver is not to blame and the receiver is an innocent victim.[1] The belief in evil eye opens up a larger discussion surrounding the nature and role of folk religion and healing in Latina spirituality. It is significant to note that belief in evil eye arrived in Latin America, and consequently on U.S. shores, through Spanish folk Catholicism. This is not the case for all of the elements of Latina spirituality that are perhaps understood as "border" practices on the fringes of dominant Roman Catholic spirituality. Belief in *curanderas*, spirits and the mixture of African and indigenous religious elements in Latina Catholicism challenge our understandings of authentic versus bogus practices. Faith healers, or *curanderas,* are spiritual healers, usually women, within Latina communities whom individuals visit when someone falls ill who cannot be cured by traditional medicine or when an illness is suspected to have spiritual origins. Though the Catholic church condemns the practice of visiting *curanderas*, many Catholic Latinas in the U.S. continue this practice that has its roots in Latin America. They do so either ignorantly or because of a sense that the church does not understand the role and significance of this cultural tradition.

Latina spirituality represents a vital dimension of the American church. The face of the global Catholic church is changing, and in fifty years the majority of the world's Catholics will be found in the southern or "Two-Thirds" World. Latinas serve as bridge people between the North and the South. They open the door for U.S. Catholics to the broader church, which is overwhelmingly brown and poor. With current issues such as illegal immigration dividing this nation, Latinas give a human face to what are often abstract political discussions. Latinas also represent the new face of Catholicism (and Christianity as a whole) in the twenty-first century. This Catholicism is increasingly Spirit driven, symbolic and devotional. For Latina Catholics, the symbolic (whether through devotion to a particular apparition of Mary or participation in a *Via Crucis*) is a privileged means to the divine and often has political implications. When Latinas locate the sacred in the everyday, spirituality saturates every aspect of their lives. Through their spirituality, Latinas lament their struggles and sufferings while simultaneously celebrating their full humanity as created in God's image.

It is estimated that by 2030 the U.S. Catholic church will be close to 80 percent Hispanic. This will change the entire nature and face of the church in the United States and signals a larger global transformation in Catholicism. The church of Rome will no longer be overwhelmingly white and European; Asia, Africa and Latin America will become the new centers of Catholicism. This trend in Catholicism marks a broader transformation in Christianity as a whole. By 2050 only one-fifth of the world's Christians will be non-Hispanic whites. This trend has been ignored by the mass media, the academy and, some would argue, by the Christian denominations themselves. For too long

European Christianity has been equated with "authentic" or normative, Christianity. The Europeanization of Christianity is perhaps best seen in Jesus imagery, which is overwhelmingly European and Euro-American. As a result, the spirituality and religiosity of Latinas are often categorized as "ethnic" or "cultural," which is a way to label them as somehow deviant.

Inculturated Catholicism and Syncretism

One of the most beautiful aspects of the Catholic faith is the manner in which it becomes shaped and transformed by its cultural setting. This process of inculturation, in which Christianity adapts to, and influences, the cultural context in which it takes root, leads to the diversity within the church. One of my favorite historical examples of inculturation is found in Augustine's classic spiritual memoir *The Confessions*. Toward the end of this autobiographical confession of faith and account of his conversion to Christianity, Augustine tells of the time in Milan with his mother Monica. Augustine and his mother are North African, and I imagine the change from what is present-day Algeria to Italy must have been quite a shock to them. Monica, a devout Catholic, is enraptured by the local bishop, Ambrose, someone who will also figure prominently in Augustine's conversion. Ambrose, however, is not so thrilled with Monica, or at least with one dimension of Monica's faith. According to African Catholic custom, offerings of food and wine were brought to shrines in honor of the saints and the dead. This practice was emphatically prohibited by Ambrose. Monica eventually grew to accept Ambrose's ban. In other words, this popular practice, which was entirely acceptable in her home African church was not allowed in Italy. This brief episode gives us a window into the question of inculturation and the fact that even in the fourth century, the church was struggling with the tension between its broader identity and its more localized expressions.

Other examples of contemporary inculturated Christianity are found in the following sections on Mary, popular religion and the *Via*

Crucis. All religious practices are inculturated. Since we human beings exist within culture, we cannot strip ourselves of our cultural markers. And why would we? The diversity of humanity's cultural expressions is a gift, not a burden. The question of inculturation is one that has become especially prominent for immigrant communities in the United States. While this has been most recently highlighted in terms of Latin American immigrants, Italians, Irish and Haitian Roman Catholics have all struggled with their cultural identity and how it is transformed in the U.S. context. One of my favorite books by a Latina author on this topic is Esmeralda Santiago's *When I Was Puerto Rican.* This memoir describes Santiago's move from Puerto Rico to New York (technically a migration, since Puerto Ricans are U.S. citizens) and how she struggled to maintain her "Puerto-Rican-ness" on the mainland. For Santiago, the more she became accepted in the U.S., the less Puerto Rican she felt. This is a sentiment many immigrants share, for as they become more comfortable in their new homes, they become alienated from their homelands.

There is, however, a fine line between inculturation and syncretism. Syncretism refers to the mixing of two or more religious traditions, often forming a new religion. While this is in fact a fairly natural process in the formation of all religions, the accusation of syncretism is sometimes used to downplay the significance of a religious belief or practice or to condemn a religious practice as heretical. In a sense all religions are syncretic, and there is no such thing as a pure religion. For example, Christianity began as a Jewish sect and still draws heavily from the Hebrew Scriptures. Within contemporary Latina culture, the question of syncretism is raised when Catholic Latinas dabble in religious beliefs and practices that are not Catholic and that are at times even condemned by the church. However, for many Latinas, these are everyday practices that are part of their religious world. My story of my son's evil eye is an example of this. My mother-in-law is a devout Catholic, and yet she sent me and my son to an indigenous faith healer, the *curandera*. My mother-in-law does not see this as a conflict with her Catholic beliefs, yet for the institutional church it is. There are historical roots to the mixing of these practices that can be traced to the conquest of the Americas, the indigenous cultures that continued to thrive in spite of Spanish rule, the transatlantic slave trade and the clergy shortage in Latin America. While the Catholic church was, and still is, a strong cultural force in Latin America, institutionally it has always been weak. There have never been enough priests to meet the needs of the population. Therefore, in that vacuum you see Catholicism inculturated, or some would say syncretized, with indigenous and African beliefs and practices. Latinas and Latin Americans are not alone in this, and I am sure that in your own faith life there may be little rituals or talismans that aren't 100 percent Catholic and that you may or may not feel guilty about when you tap into that dimension of your spirituality.

The People's Faith

The site where the inculturated dimension of Catholicism is most obviously revealed has been described as popular or lived religion. Popular religious practices are local religious expressions that are definitively marked by their cultural context. Unlike the Mass or the sacraments, which are highly formalized and consequently regulated by the church hierarchy, popular religious practices reflect the faith of the people and the manner in which they make Catholicism their own. Perhaps no other Latino theologian has emphasized the centrality of popular religion more than Cuban-American Orlando Espín. He views popular religion as a core religious expression within Latina communities. His writings cover various themes, the most significant of which is his work on popular religion as an expression of tradition.

When I was growing up my parents dragged us to the shrine of Our Lady of Charity (the patron saint of Cuba) in Miami on her feast day, September 8. We would often bring yellow flowers to Mass and my parents would have a chance to reconnect with many friends they saw only on that one day. When my brother and I were old enough to start complaining about this excursion, noting when September 8 was not on a Sunday and therefore questioning the "extra" Mass, my parents would respond that we had to go. When pressed they would answer, "Because it is tradition." Traditions, especially religious traditions, are ways in which we construct our identity, drawing from the past in order to speak to the present. While Catholics speak of the Catholic Tradition in a monolithic way, that tradition is in fact made up of many traditions that throughout the ages have shaped Catholicism in its local contexts. Traditions are passed on. They are dynamic and alive. We pick and choose those traditions that are important to us and transmit them to our children, our peers and our communities. My parents raised me in a world that was saturated with Cuban culture. Thus, we have many traditions that flesh out our Cuban identity. However, I will not necessarily pass on all of these traditions to my children. Some I reject because I find them too hierarchical and patriarchal, others because they speak to the Cuba of my parents' past and not the future I envision for my Cuban-Guatemalan-American children.

Espín sees popular religion as an important bearer of tradition. In addition to the tradition of the church—the official teachings and documents—there is the tradition that incorporates the traditions of everyday laypeople who do not necessarily have a voice in the hierarchical church. The traditions and the Tradition exist in a dynamic relationship with each other, and together they form Catholic identity in its various cultural contexts. The laity thus participates in the construction of Catholic identity. It is not just something that is handed down to us that we accept uncritically. This is vital for the spirituality of Latinas, for it recognizes their role in the "tradition-ing" (passing on) of religious identity within their families and communities. As noted above, Latinas are the bearers of culture and religion in their families. In highlighting the way in which the everyday, lived, popular faith of Latinas contributes to Catholic tradition and identity, Espín recognizes the vital role of Latina spirituality within Catholic identity.

In addition to describing popular religion as a bearer of tradition, Espín also sees it as an authentic expression of what theologians call the *sensus fidelium*. The *sensus fidelium* can best be described as the "faithfull intuition" of the people. While the canon of Scripture is written and fixed, Espín wants us to realize that tradition is a living reality. He sees "the *living witness and faith* of the Christian people," to be "just as important as the written texts of Tradition (or, in fact, more important)."[2] In other words, and here I agree strongly with Espín, the faithfull witness of the Catholic laity must be recognized as a vital and dynamic source for understanding Catholic identity. To emphasize our common faith-full intuition is to highlight the ways in which all Catholics participate in and contribute to Catholic faith. Popular religion is a "cultural expression" of the *sensus fidelium*. This theme will be explored concretely below, where I emphasize the everyday religious practices of Latinas as a source for Catholic spirituality.

For Espín, this *sensus fidelium* is infallible, for its origin is the Holy Spirit who works in the Christian community throughout history. Also, this *sensus fidelium* is always expressed in a context building on the symbols and language of a particular community. My parents' devotion to Our Lady of Charity is a perfect example. She is a cultural expression of Catholicism as the patron saint of Cuba. My parents' particular devotion to her (the flowers, the shrine, the feast day) and the official expression of Catholicism (the Mass) come together. Devotion to Our Lady of Charity is not required of all Catholics, yet it is a Cuban way of being Catholic. Her feast day is not a holy day of obligation, yet for Cuban Catholics a visit to her shrine on her feast day is virtually obligatory.

Espín does not propose noncritical acceptance of the Spirit working within Christians. He offers three criteria by which to judge whether an expression of the *sensus fidelium* is just: Scripture, the written texts of tradition and the historical and sociological contexts from which the tradition comes. In other words, the reliability of the faithfull intuition of the people of God does not include bypassing the need for discernment. There must be a dynamic dialogue between hierarchical, historical and lay-initiated dimensions of Catholicism. Underlying Espín's assertion that popular religion is an expression of the *sensus fidelium* is the question, "Who are the bearers (subjects) of tradition?" In my example, it is my parents who are the bearers of tradition. The *sensus fidelium* is always expressed through the context of the faithful, whether symbolically or linguistically. Popular religion is a primary site of this expression. However, we must be aware of the human limitations of popular religion. Like the church, the faith of the people is guided by the Spirit, though always limited by our humanity. In other words, our human expressions of humanity's encounter with the divine are always limited. No prayer, liturgy or ritual can embody God in God's fullness. We are always, ultimately, at a loss for words to describe the height, depth, width and breadth of the sacred.

From Espín emerges a vision of popular religion as a bearer of Catholic tradition, a vital source for an ecclesiology that wants to take seriously a theology of the laity. To emphasize the authority of the laity as bearers and transmitters of tradition is to acknowledge what has gone on throughout the history of Catholicism. Religion does not exist exclusively in papal documents and academic theological texts. It lives in the people who embrace and celebrate their faith. This emphasis on the laity's faithful intuition is vital for a Latina spirituality. Latinas have very few avenues to an authoritative voice in ecclesial structures. They are however, religious authorities. In embracing the *sensus fidelium* operating in Latina spirituality, their theological authority is affirmed. This is powerful for all women, who are sadly excluded from participation in the official power of ecclesial structures. However, in celebrating ourselves as bearers of tradition we acknowledge our authority as members of the church. The fact that Latinas are most often the bearers and transmitters of religion and cultural values—a role they share with many other women—is affirmed through the *sensus*. In my home I may have learned the official teachings of Catholicism through my Sunday school classes (all taught by women, by the way), but it is from my mother and grandmother that I learned to *be* religious, how to infuse it in my being. The *sensus fidelium* offers a window into the impact of the everyday faith formation women command and their role in the "tradition-ing" of Catholicism in all its cultural diversity.

The Globalized Church

Recognizing the diversity of Catholic expressions forces us to acknowledge the true global face of the church. We currently live in an age that is characterized by globalization, the interconnectedness of all humanity. Whether through technology, communications, politics or trade, the world as we know it is more interconnected than it has been at any point in human history. From the Roman Catholic standpoint, globalization is not an unmixed blessing. John Paul II wrote, "Globalization, *a priori*, is neither good or nor bad. It will be what people make of it."[3] On the positive end of the spectrum we find an emphasis on: increased oneness of world, information that is more democratically available, and more prolific human rights language. However, a negative assessment highlights the following: insensitivity to human suffering (the victims of globalization), inattention to ecological sustainability, polarization between cultures (who has access to what), and the disempowerment of the state (in other words the political clout of multinational corporations and their influence on global economies). We must also remember the ambiguous legacy of the historical, colonial era of globalization, where the missionary enterprise accompanied European expansion in dubious ways.

A Catholic response to globalization must ground itself in the Catholic social teaching, valuing the equality of all humans as God's children. It must emphasize the dignity of the human person, a vision grounded in our shared *imago Dei*. We must also focus on the social nature of the human. We are communal and relational in nature. Foundational here is the idea of the common good, which must be central to society. Solidarity and the preferential option for the poor must ground the attention we give to the particular struggles of the poor. For poor Latinas, this solidarity is vital as they struggle in their daily lives to provide for their families. The poor must be our foundation for the prophetic denouncement of the structures that create the often silent victims of globalization. Special attention must also be given to the homogenizing force of globalization, where the diverse cultures are assimilated and subsumed under a dominant Western ethos.

In other words, in this newly globalized world the influence and impact of U.S. culture is startling. Living in an indigenous town in Guatemala, I was shocked to be confronted daily by Old Navy T-shirts (fake, mind you), popular U.S. shows on television and Pepsi everywhere. I witnessed indigenous youth reject the traditional Mayan dress that their ancestors have worn since before colonial times, in favor of Western jeans and T-shirts. The art of weaving with a back-strap loom, which Mayan women have done in the same way for over a thousand years, is now being lost as fewer girls want to learn to weave. They would rather dress like the U.S. teens they see on television than like their mothers, grandmothers and ancestors. This emphasis on dress may seem like a mere nod to pop culture. However, if you look closely, you discover that, depending on one's hometown, there are different patterns and animals woven into blouses, and all of these tell the cosmological story of each particular community. Therefore to reject traditional dress is to reject your culture and a piece of your Mayan soul.

This homogenizing trend goes against the catholicity of the church, which emphasizes unity in diversity. The catholicity of the church refers to its universality, its presence throughout the globe. However, catholicity does not imply homogeneity. Instead, the catholicity of Catholicism speaks to its ability to flourish in different contexts. Catholicity refers to its universality within, not in spite of, its diversity. This trend toward Western homogeneity also goes against the lived reality of the church, which is increasingly globalized and non-Western. With the growth of a more southern (African and Latin

American) church comes a different understanding of Catholicism, a different sense of Catholic spirituality.

We find in these areas the growth of a more Spirit-focused (some would say conservative) spirituality that is clearly seen in the growth of charismatic Catholicism. This ecclesial model, which is radically different from the liberation theology that is often associated with Latin America, needs our careful study and attention. I think about this often when I work with Latina communities here and in Guatemala. More and more I encounter Catholics who are turning to charismatic Catholicism and even leaving the church and joining Pentecostal and evangelical denominations. It is in these settings that they find a more Spirit-focused, conservative spirituality that speaks to them in profound ways. Part of the appeal is found in the avenues for lay leadership in these Christian groups, especially when they draw from the local community. Another appealing factor is the attention these groups give to everyday struggles (such as alcoholism or marital problems) in their worship settings.

Attention to the globalized church forces us to think more broadly about the church here in the United States. In my eyes it is no longer useful to speak of a northern or southern church but instead of an American church that embraces all of the Americas. This is not a revolutionary statement. Whether one looks at John Paul II's 1999 apostolic exhortation *Ecclesia in America* or economic and cultural analyses of globalization, the porous nature of national borders is our reality.

The question of legal and illegal immigration brings up a different set of issues, though one that also needs our careful attention. A Latina spirituality places these issues, among many others, at the forefront of Catholic thought. As Catholics, we cannot ignore the plight of twelve million illegal immigrants in the United States, most of them Latin American and Catholic, and not have a thoughtful discussion about a Catholic response to this reality. This has profound implications for how we view the church and our participation within it. It forces us to ponder deeply the meaning of "love thy neighbor" and "hospitality to the foreigner in our midst"—two challenging biblical teachings for our spirituality. The mission where I was based in Guatemala received close to two thousand visitors from the United States. These church groups and university students would spend a week at the mission, volunteering in the various projects and supporting the work of the church. A key emphasis of this program is cultivating a global sense of solidarity and awareness of the issues and concerns that mark this small community. The parish priests wanted visitors from the U.S. to recognize this Mayan community as their community, this Mayan church as their church. This was not a strategy to erase differences, but a manner of building bridges across the church of the Americas. As we turn now to some specific Latina devotions, I hope more such bridges are built and that we all find some spiritual nourishment in the everyday faith of Latina spirituality.

FOOD FOR THOUGHT

1. What are some examples of "folk Catholicism"—such as belief in the evil eye—in your cultural background?
2. How does your everyday spirituality shape your relationship with the sacred?
3. What are some of your own personal popular religious practices?

Prayer for the American Church

Invocation:

Loving Spirit, guide us.

Wise Spirit, teach us.

Just Spirit, empower us.

Scripture: The Unnamed Concubine: Judges 19

Response: Let us pray for those who suffer innocently and unjustly on a daily basis.

Hear the cries of exploited women who suffer in silence.

Let us pray for the courage to recognize that our neighbor is not merely she who is near us or like us.

Recognize the beauty and diversity of God's creation.

Let us pray for the vision to see God's presence in rituals that seem foreign to us.

See the faith of our southern sisters and brothers.

CHAPTER THREE

• MARIAN DEVOTION •

Sonia stood in front of Cachita's (Our Lady of Charity's) altar clutching sunflowers in her sweaty hand. As she stared at the small statue, bathed in fine linens and gold, she focused on the small, brown face, so much like her own. The mural of Cuban heroes on the wall behind Cachita (mostly men) blurred out of focus. "Please," she pleaded silently, "do not let me lose another child.... My husband will leave me if I miscarry again." She stared at Cachita's face, trying to find some comfort. She slowly walked over to the white plastic buckets at the side of the altar and placed her flowers in the overflowing bins. "I promise to bring you flowers every day for a year if I deliver this child." With that *promesa,* she left the shrine silently, passing a dozen or so women praying silently in the pews.

A fundamental hallmark of Latina spirituality is the centrality of Mary. Latinas have found a sacred *hermana* in the various apparition stories of Mary in the Americas. Through their devotion to Mary, Latinas relate their everyday problems and struggles to the sacred. Latina Marian devotion is fundamental for understanding Latina spirituality, a spirituality marked by the presence of the sacred in the everyday. In Mary, Latinas find a mother and sister who accompanies them, a woman who understands their family concerns. Like Mary, whose son was not born in luxurious surroundings, poor Latina women identify with the struggles Mary faced as a young mother. Her Magnificat speaks to her accompaniment of Latinas in their poverty. Mary's flight to Egypt with her husband and young son speak to the immigration experience of so many Latinas. Latina Marian devotions are also clearly marked by their cultural particularity. Through her Latin American apparitions, Mary assumes the face and the cultural particularity of the community in which she appears. In Cuba and Mexico, devotions to Our Lady of Charity and Our Lady of Guadalupe exemplify this Marian spirituality. While devotions to these two *virgenes* (Spanish for virgin, a term Latinas use to refer to Marian apparitions and statues generally) are strongly shaped by their cultural context, they represent universal devotions all Catholic women can embrace.

La Caridad del Cobre—Our Lady of Charity

Our Lady of Charity, known in Spanish as *La Caridad del Cobre,* is the patron saint of Cuba. She is the most prominent and visible sign of Cuban identity in communities both on and off the island. Cachita, as many Cubans affectionately call *La Caridad,* represents Cuban national and racial identity, and on her feast day, September 8, thousands of devotees crowd her shrines in Cuba and Miami, bearing yellow flowers for her. The exact date of her apparition is unclear, but scholars agree that she appeared sometime in the first quarter of the seventeenth century. The first historical document of her account is a 1687 narrative by Juan Moreno, one of the three men to discover her statue. As he recounts it, Moreno, an African slave, was with the indigenous brothers Rodrigo de Hoyos and Juan de Hoyos gathering salt in the bay of Nipe. The three men saw a statue floating in the water and thought it was a bird. Upon closer inspection they discovered that it was a statue of Mary engraved with the words *"Yo Soy La Virgen de la Caridad,"* ("I am the Virgin of Charity"). They pulled the statue onto their boat, noting that miraculously, her clothes were dry.

The three men took the statue to Spanish authorities in the town of Cobre, a copper mining community of royal slaves to which Juan Moreno belonged. An altar for her was constructed near the slave barracks. Miracles began to be attributed to her. Individuals were healed, and the statue began to mysteriously disappear and appear throughout the night, always returning with her clothes wet. When Spanish authorities tried to move her altar to a more "worthy" place far from the slave barracks, she protested by reappearing at her original altar near the slaves. In 1613 she was moved to El Cobre, where she remains today. She was placed on the main altar of the shrine in El Cobre in 1640.

It was not until the latter half of the nineteenth century that devotion to *La Caridad* spread throughout Cuba. Prior to that, she remained a local devotion in a community of slaves and ex-slaves. However, during Cuba's wars for independence from Spain, soldiers appealed to *La Caridad* or wore her image on their uniforms. The altar of her shrine is covered with soldiers' uniforms, medals and crutches that attest to healings. By the time Cuba won its independence, *La Caridad* had become the national virgin, *la Virgin Mambisa* (Fierce Virgin). In 1915 a group of veterans petitioned the Vatican to make her patroness of the island and in 1916 Benedict XV named her patroness and a new shrine was constructed for her.

As devotion to *La Caridad* spread throughout the island, however, her image and narrative changed to fit the needs of the young Cuban nation. If you visit her image in Cuba or its duplicate in Miami, you are confronted with a copper skinned Mary with dark hair wearing an elaborate gold and white dress and a crown. What you do not realize from viewing this elaborate image is that beneath the dress there is no body, just a wooden stick with a head. This original image of *La Caridad* is radically different from the images you see among contemporary Cubans and Cuban Americans. Most often this image of Mary is dressed in blue (Mary's traditional color) looming large over three men. The three men, known popularly as the three Juans, are on a rowboat with waves crashing over it. One of the men is Black, one Caucasian and the third is perhaps biracial. The Black man is on his knees in prayer. These three Juans represent the three dominant races and cultures of Cuba—African, Spanish and the biracial mixture of

African and Spanish. This is often the story and the image of *La Caridad* that you encounter today.

Why the change? As her devotion spread, the narrative and imagery of *La Caridad* shifted to meet the needs of the Cuban population at large. She became, in a sense, more Cuban. The historical story of *La Caridad* is a story of a Marian image that appears to, and accompanies, the slave and indigenous communities in Cobre. When the Spanish Captain in charge of the Cobre slave mines, Antonio Sánchez de Moya, orders a new shrine to be built on a quarry hill away from the mines, *La Caridad* protests. She sends lights in the sky and is eventually returned to her desired space next to the mines. She thus moves from the marginalized (in her apparition) to the centers of power and back to the marginalized (the miners). However, as her devotion moves from its exclusively Afro-Cuban context to that of all Cuban people, her story is adapted. The three men in the boat become representative of all Cubans, and instead of a long narrative telling the story of the various miracles associated with her in a slave community, we are given this image of a miraculous apparition over a stormy sea.

In many ways this should not surprise us. Symbols and images, whether religious or not, are constantly shaped and transformed by the communities that value them. As cultural manifestations of humanity's encounter with the sacred, religious symbols naturally reflect the contours and historicity of human culture. It also should not surprise us that an image of Mary appearing to three men struggling in a boat during a storm became so significant to the Cuban people. After all, an image of Mary who appears to men in a boat speaks strongly to a community that has had thousands of loved ones arrive in this country in boats themselves. A community who has lost thousands of loved ones to the raging waters of the Atlantic is drawn to an image of Mary who appears to three men during a storm. For Cuban-American Latinas, *La Caridad* is a Cuban manifestation of Mary that represents God's preferential option for their community. Devotion to *La Caridad* extends well beyond the walls of her shrine and is found in the various home and yard altars that dot Cuban-American homes. Many forms of popular devotion center on her, most notably instrumental and healing prayers.

The provocative 1994 Cuban film *Fresa y Chocolate* (*Strawberry and Chocolate*) tells the story of an unlikely friendship that develops between a gay Cuban teacher and a Marxist student. Diego, the teacher, is a strong devotee of *La Caridad del Cobre*. He is constantly bringing yellow flowers to the statue of *La Caridad*, having conversations with her, and pleading with her to help him with his love life. His neighbor Nancy is devoted to Saint Barbara and carries on a similar relationship with her, threatening to stick her statue in a closet if the man she loves does not fall for her. When things do not go Diego's way, he threatens to punish *La Caridad*. The rantings of a crazy man and woman? Far from it. Diego's devotion represents a very Cuban way of relating to Cachita—she is seen as confidante and friend. Cuban women often come to *La Caridad* with prayers concerning love, romance and marriage. She is associated with conception and childbirth. *Promesas* are often made to her. A *promesa* involves making a petition to Mary or a saint and promising to follow up with an action if the prayer is granted. Since *La Caridad*'s favorite color is yellow, yellow flowers and candles dot her shrines. In bringing her flowers and purchasing the color of candles that please her, as well as in the conversational way women often speak to *La Caridad*, a relational and sacramental Latina spirituality is revealed. The statues of *La Caridad* are not merely representations, they reveal her presence in this community.

These friendships with Mary and the saints are part of a spirituality that millions of Latinas share, a spirituality that provides a wonderful model for all women. Here the sacred is not a detached, hierarchical reality but is instead part of one's everyday life. Mary and the saints are not dead in the sense of being absent or forgotten. They are not lifeless statues to Latinas. They are alive in their relationships with their devotees. There is a dynamic reciprocity at the center of these relationships. This type of spirituality is built on a very sacramental way of relating to the sacred, a hallmark of Catholicism. The statues of Mary and the saints are not mere representations of these individuals, they *are* these individuals in a very tangible way. The statues participate in what they represent. This sacramental worldview is more than belief in the seven sacraments. It also encompasses an understanding of the world as infused with God's grace, the giftedness of God's love. For example, Catholics, unlike their Protestant brothers and sisters, maintain that through the eucharistic prayer at Mass transubstantiation occurs—the bread and wine are literally transformed into the Body and Blood of Jesus. This belief highlights the sacramental nature of the Catholic worldview in which symbols do not merely represent but also participate in that which they symbolize. The statue of *La Caridad* I have on my altar at home is not just a beautiful sculpture to me. I respect it as if it were *La Caridad* herself. That is why I care for the statue, pray to it and light candles to it. This is not, I would argue, an exclusively Latina practice, though it is perhaps more integrated into our spirituality. Is what I am discussing so radically different from lighting a candle before a statue in church? When you light that candle, is it for the statue or for the saint and the grace she or he embodies that is sacramentally represented in that statue?

Our Lady of Guadalupe

Devotion to Our Lady of Guadalupe is another Marian face of Latina spirituality. Guadalupe is the largest and most widespread Marian devotion in Latin America and among U.S. Latinas. Yet, her patronage expands well beyond these communities. In 1999 John Paul II named her patroness of the Americas in his apostolic exhortation *Ecclesia in America*. However, the heart of her story and most of her devotees remain within Mexican communities across the globe. For Mexican and Mexican-American women, Guadalupe is a liberating and empowering feminine symbol. For the Mexican people as a whole, she represents their cultural and religious identity. As a people born of the blood of the conquered and the conqueror, Guadalupe represents the birth of a new people, a *mestizo* Mexican people who are a mixture of both indigenous and Spanish cultures. In the bleakest moment in Mexican history, the conquest, Guadalupe appeared to bring a message of hope and love to the Mexican community.

Our Lady of Guadalupe appeared in 1531 on the mountain of Tepeyac to the indigenous man Juan Diego. Juan Diego, a convert to Christianity, was walking to Mass early on a Saturday morning when he heard some beautiful music. He then heard a voice calling him. He walked up the hillside, drawn to the voice. At the top of the hill, he encountered a beautiful lady, radiant with love and compassion. She identified herself as the Mother of God, mother of creation, who had come in response to the cries of those in the Americas who called to her in their suffering. She then ordered Juan Diego to go to the bishop to request that a shrine be built in her honor on the site of her apparition. Juan Diego protested, claiming he was a nothing, unworthy of the bishop's attention or this important message. Guadalupe assured him that he was the one chosen for this task. The bishop, as Juan Diego predicted, did not believe him, and the next day he returned and reported his failure to her. She sent him back to the bishop, who remained unconvinced and demanded a sign as proof.

Juan Diego tries to avoid encountering Guadalupe again. He has failed in his task and his uncle is also very ill. However, he cannot avoid her. Guadalupe assures him that his uncle will be healed, and then instructs Juan Diego to go gather roses on the hillside as proof of her apparition. Since this is winter in the desert, these flowers truly are a miracle. Juan Diego gathers the flowers in his cloak and goes to the bishop. The bishops' servants recognize Juan Diego from his earlier visit and attempt to block his entry. However, the intoxicating smell of the roses convinces them to allow Juan Diego to enter and see the bishop. In order to present the flowers to him, Juan Diego opens his cloak and as the flowers fall to the floor the image of Guadalupe miraculously appears on his cloak. This is the image that hangs in her Basilica outside of Mexico City.

The narrative of Guadalupe's apparition raises various important themes that are fundamental for understanding Latina spirituality. In the narrative, she appears to Juan Diego, a self proclaimed "lowly" indigenous man who sees little worth in himself. We must remember that this apparition occurred during the bloodiest moment in Mexican history, the conquest. In the midst of the bloodshed and trauma of an indigenous community who is having its entire universe overturned, we have a story about Mary's preferential option for the marginalized, a story of flowers and song. Surely, if Guadalupe wanted her shrine built immediately, the most efficient and appropriate means to communicate this would have been to appear before the bishop. He is, after all, the one who has official authority in transmitting the gospel. However, in this story Guadalupe empowers Juan Diego with the gospel message. It is he, the indigenous man, who brings Mary's message of love to the bishop. In a moment when the Catholic church is imposing the forced conversion of thousands of indigenous men, women and children, we find an indigenous man converting the bishop to Mary's message. He becomes the bearer of the gospel.

Guadalupe's apparition to Juan Diego reminds us that the gospel message often comes from unlikely sources and that we must never pre-judge based on the messenger. It forces us to ask ourselves if we ever play the role assigned to the bishop in the story—denying God's message. When have we chosen not to hear? When have we judged someone as unworthy of the gospel? The Johannine account of Jesus' encounter with the Samaritan woman teaches a similar lesson (John 4:1–42). When they see Jesus conversing with a Samaritan woman, the disciples are shocked that he would speak to a woman who belongs to a group Jews see as ritually impure. Jesus not only talks to her, but also empowers her with the gospel message.

I think about this story often, given my role as a scholar of religion with an academic degree that legitimates my voice. However, one does not need a PH.D. to live and transmit the good news. In fact, it is often the everyday, uneducated, grassroots people I have encountered through my work who have truly taught me the most important lessons about spirituality. Guadalupe does not want her shrine in the city but on the mountainside, away from the centers of power. Tepeyac is a sacred site for the Aztecs, associated with the Aztec goddess Tonantzin. Mary reminds us that the gospel not only comes from unlikely sources but can also appear in unlikely places. We cannot assume that if we build a church God's presence will become manifest. Sometimes the sacred appears on a mountainside. Unlike many images of Mary, such as *La Caridad*, where Mary is carrying the baby Jesus, this image of Mary is pregnant. The simple black cord around her waist, an indigenous marker of pregnancy, reveals her condition. As with *La Caridad*, we find women's devotions and petitions to Guadalupe related to issues of motherhood and pregnancy.

Guadalupe's feast day is December 12. In Roman Catholic parishes throughout the Americas, but especially in areas with large Mexican populations, celebrations begin at dawn. The celebration traditionally begins with the singing of *Mañanitas*, literally translated "early morning tunes" sung in her honor. They are sung outside of the church and are often accompanied by mariachis. The timing is significant for it is in remembrance of her first appearance to Juan Diego at dawn. After the singing, celebrants enter the church and celebrate Mass in her honor. A second significant dimension of the celebration is the reenactment of her apparition. Usually after the homily (if reenacted during Mass), this retelling of her apparition reveals its significance for the Mexican-American community. Through reenacting her encounters with Juan Diego and the miracles surrounding it, the community affirms her presence among them and her accompaniment of them in their struggles. The personal encounter of Guadalupe with Juan Diego is highlighted. She is not merely a statue or an image that is venerated; through the retelling of her encounters with Juan Diego, the community reaffirms their encounters, and thus their relationship with her. The story remains alive to the community even today; she continues to appear to them through their faith and devotions.

In his classic epic *Rain of Gold*, Victor Villaseñor tells the cross-generational story of his Mexican family and their lives in Mexico and the United States. One of the most colorful characters in the novel is his grandmother, who arises each morning, goes to the bathroom in their latrine, smokes a cigarette and has a conversation with Our Lady of Guadalupe. What seems like an irreverent act is actually a testament to the faith of his grandmother and her sacramental worldview in which the sacred is interwoven into every moment of her daily life. Her daily conversations with Guadalupe, during arguably the most private act a person does in his or her daily routine, demonstrates the intimacy she feels with *La Virgen*. His grandmother offers a model of spirituality from which many of us could learn. I am not necessarily suggesting that we all start praying in the bathroom, but maybe some of us should. Our spiritual encounters do not have to be appointments we make with God, set apart like a visit to the doctor. Our spirituality should saturate every task we do. We should be ready to encounter the sacred at every moment. Juan Diego was not expecting to encounter the mother of God that Saturday morning, but he did.

Perhaps one of the most poignant accounts I have read regarding Guadalupan devotion was told by my friend and colleague Nancy Pineda-Madrid, who described an incident she witnessed in her twenties when she living in Chihuahua, Mexico. Celebrating the feast day of Guadalupe in a poor desert town, Nancy describes the scene at the church, noting that the traditional practice of singing to Guadalupe was well under way, with devotees bringing plastic flowers as offerings (it was all that they could afford and was available), when a mysterious group of women arrived. These women, whom Nancy had never seen before, arrived with their arms full of fragrant, fresh roses. "Who are they?" she asked. "*Cantineras*," she is informed, prostitutes who spend their days locked up in cantinas selling their bodies to men from the U.S. who cross the border to be with them. These women make arrangements to have the flowers brought for Guadalupe from out of town and are given permission by local police to emerge in order to honor her. They are, Nancy discovers, extremely poor women who become prostitutes in order to care for their families. As Nancy reminds us, "Their presence on the feast of Guadalupe served as an annual reminder of the egregious injustices wreaked upon poor people, especially upon poor women." However, Nancy muses, their presence in their church on Guadalupe's feast day is a cry and protest against these injustices, for "with their presence in church the *cantineras* publicly professed their own human dignity, a dignity they could affirm through Guadalupe."[1] This moving account reminds us of how Latina Marian spirituality is a source for women's dignity and empowerment.

Marianismo and Latina Marian Empowerment

Like *La Caridad del Cobre*, Guadalupe is a brown skinned virgin who represents the clash and mixture of cultures that constitute the Americas: European, indigenous and African. For Latinas, these Marian apparitions represent their culture and their struggles. She appears within their context and accompanies them throughout the joys and heartaches of life. Latinas relate to these images of Mary and find comfort in them. They identify with these images of Mary as a mother who has some understanding of their daily lives. Both La Caridad and Guadalupe not only appeared in these Latin American contexts, they remained within them. The image of Guadalupe in the basilica is the same image that appeared miraculously before the bishop and Juan Diego. The statue of *La Caridad* in her shrine in Cuba is the same statue that was gathered from the bay of Nipe. Both *La Caridad* and Guadalupe, as well as other apparitions and devotions to Mary throughout Latin America, represent a cultural manifestation of the sacred in Latin American eyes. This is especially important for Latinas in the United States. Torn from their home countries, often with their families divided, devotions such as *La Caridad* and Guadalupe accompany Latinas in the United States and remain as constant reminders of their homelands or the lands of their parents' heritage. Guadalupe and *La Caridad* also remind all of us of the brown face of the American church and the ambiguous history of Catholicism in the Americas, where slave and indigenous stories are placed at the forefront of these apparitions.

Latinas, however, do not uncritically accept the image of Mary. While she is a symbol of strength, culture and empowerment, there is also an awareness of the manner in which Mary has been used to promote unrealistic stereotypes about motherhood. Indeed, as a virgin-mother, Mary represents an unattainable ideal for any woman. Too often this is framed in a virgin-whore dichotomy where women are labeled as either pure, virginal Marys or promiscuous Eves. This leads to the Latin American and Latina stereotype of *Marianismo*. *Marianismo* places women on a pedestal, arguing that in their chasteness and purity they are superior to men. Any woman who falls short of this ideal is quickly disregarded as a fallen and tainted woman. As colorfully noted by Chicana writer Sandra Cisneros, "This is why I was angry for so many years every time I saw *la Virgen de Guadalupe*, my culture's role model for brown women like me. She was damn dangerous, an ideal so lofty and unrealistic it was laughable. Did boys have to aspire to be Jesus? I never saw any evidence of it."[2] The emphasis on her motherhood, which is empowering for so many Latina women, is also alien to those women who do not or cannot become mothers themselves. Cisneros's comments speak far beyond the boundaries of Latina culture. How many Catholic women are told to be pure and chaste like Mary? How many are accused of being an Eve, a betrayer, if they do not meet those unrealistic standards? Similarly, why is it that Catholic men are rarely held to such standards?

There is a long history of emphasizing Mary and the ideal of *Marianismo* which promotes a submissive model of womanhood. Mary's obedience is emphasized, and the quiet, submissive, humble Latina is celebrated. Latinas are expected to accept passively the suffering in their lives in the same way that Mary humbly accepted her role as mother of Jesus and his death. This model of Marian motherhood emphasizes self-sacrifice—the needs of the family and the larger community always come before the needs of the woman. Within the everyday lives of Latinas, this *Marianismo* can become a constricting space that limits their full humanity and resigns them to a future of humble servitude. Again, Latinas are not alone in having the obedient Mary imposed upon them as a passive ideal for women. Latinas however have been known to transform this oppressive stereotype and use it to their advantage. *Marianismo* gives women a sense of power and control in the everyday, domestic sphere. The mother often becomes the object of reverence in her home, especially in the eyes of her children and grandchildren. *Marianismo* is the flip side of *machismo*, the Spanish word that is used to describe the particular incarnation of sexism in Latina and Latin American communities. Nonetheless, a Latina spirituality must be aware of the manners in which the Marian dimension of her faith can contribute to her marginalization. A Latina spirituality offers Catholic women an empowered image of Mary that is more than the humble virgin mother.

A new generation of Latinas is taking the image of Mary and mining it as a source of their strength and sexuality. Long used to justify the stereotype of the virginal, pure woman, the image of Mary is transformed by Latina artists and writers into a symbol of female sexuality and the body. This is clearly seen in the artwork of Laura Luna and Alma Lopez. Both these artists take the images of Mary that emerge from their culture, *La Caridad* and Guadalupe, and transform them by depicting Mary as nude. They are controversial pieces that may offend some, yet their purpose is to demonstrate the sacredness of the female body. These images are also a reaction to a reduction of the body as only a site of sexual transgression. Instead, these artists argue, depicting *La Caridad* and Guadalupe as nude affirms the goodness of the human body. Some theologies treat the human body as an impediment to authentic spirituality and communion with the divine. Within this paradigm, women are most closely associated with the body and men with the mind or soul. This leads to a hierarchical privileging of men.

Through their depiction of the Marian nude, these artists speak to Latinas' discomfort with the vilification of the body. As Sandra Cisneros, whose essay inspired Alma Lopez's nude Guadalupe, writes, "When I see *la Virgen de Guadalupe* I want to lift her dress as I did my dolls' and look to see if she comes with *chones*, and does her *panocha* look like mine, and does she have dark nipples too? Yes, I am certain she does. She is not neuter like Barbie. She gave birth. She has a womb."[3] These Latinas reject the *Marianismo* ideal that presents ideal womanhood as chaste and virginal in the narrowest of senses, paradoxically maternal and submissive. They see Mary as an embodied woman whose embodiment includes a celebration of the female body. I find Cisneros's statement to be one of the most powerful I have read regarding Mary. Cisneros reminds us that Mary was a flesh and blood woman, that she physically labored and gave birth to the son of God. I think that we often forget that, and I include many Latinas in this camp. While we ask Mary's intercession for a healthy pregnancy we don't think about the fact that she gave birth, that she had a body that was holy. Authors like Cisneros and artists like Luna and Lopez remind us of the sacredness of Mary's flesh and of all women's bodies.

FOOD FOR THOUGHT

1. Reflect on either the story of Guadalupe or *La Caridad del Cobre*. How does the apparition story speak to you (or not)?
2. What does it mean to understand Guadalupe as the patroness of all the Americas?
3. Latinas recognize that Mary can serve as both a source of empowerment and oppression. Do you see Mary as either or both? What does Mary mean to you?
4. Are there ways in which devotion to Mary might enhance your sense of dignity and reverence toward your body?

PRAYER TO MARY

Invocation:

> Mother of Wisdom, inspire us.
>
> Mother of Justice, guide us.
>
> Mother of Compassion, inspire us.

Scripture: The Magnificat: Luke 1:46–55

Response: Let us ask Mary, Mother of Wisdom, to inspire us in our daily spirituality.

Wise Mother, encourage us.

Let us ask Mary, Mother of Justice, to guide us in the face of oppression.

Strong Mother, awaken us.

Let us ask Mary, Mother of Compassion, to inspire us to feel empathy for others.

Loving Mother, nurture us.

CHAPTER 4

• POPULAR RELIGION: EVERYDAY FAITH
AND THE SAINTS •

The cemetery freaked Cati out. She did not understand why they had to come here every year. She knew it was important to honor her dead grandparents, but hanging out at their graves for half the night? And the food thing...as if they were going to crawl out of their graves and eat tamales with us. She couldn't even tell her friends where she was going tonight. What would they think? Still though, she loved her grandparents and missed them a lot. Mami was always talking about how much they suffered to come to this country. Cati wondered though, would she drag her kids to the cemetery to visit her parents' graves?

As we have seen, a fundamental dimension of Latina spirituality is popular religion. In this section I want to highlight the everyday religious beliefs and practices of Latina communities. This daily faith of the people is an important starting point for theological reflection because in these lived religious practices a community's encounter with the sacred is expressed. The study of popular religion also reminds us that every expression of humanity's encounter with the divine is limited and nourished by the culture in which it appears. Often easier to describe than define, popular religion refers to a community's contextual traditions that emphasize their everyday beliefs and practices. Popular religion, however, should not be seen in opposition to what has been classified as official religion. Official religion, the religion of the dominant church, need not be in conflict with popular religion. Popular and official religious practices are meant to relate to each other, sometimes flourishing side by side, other times in tension.

The diversity of the relationship between popular and official religion is seen in devotion to *La Caridad*. The large feast day celebration and Mass in her honor is organized and supported by the Archdiocese of Miami. However, when it comes to other sorts of rituals surrounding *La Caridad*—for example her association with the African *orisha* (spirit) Oshun—the official church is not as supportive and, in fact, is in direct opposition. This association of Oshun with *La Caridad* occurred as a result of the mixture of African religion and Catholicism during the colonial slave era in Cuba. Slaves often "hid" their devotion to their African spirits behind images of Catholic saints. They pretended to participate in Catholic worship, when in fact they were worshipping their spirits. Because of these practices, certain saints and images of Mary, even today, are associated with particular *orishas*.

My emphasis on popular religion is meant to provide insight into Latina spiritual practices that can serve as complements to official rituals. The study of popular religion is especially important for the spirituality of Latinas. In fact, the study of Latina spirituality would be impossible without careful attention to popular religion. Excluded from traditional avenues of leadership in public, official religion, popular religion is the primary way to access the lived faith of Latinas as it interweaves with their everyday lives. At times popular religion and official ritual are in tension; at times they intersect.

One of the best-known novels by a Cuban-American, Cristina García's *Dreaming in Cuban*, tells the story of Cuban exiles from the perspectives of four women: those who remained in Cuba, represented by Celia and Felicia; those who came in the 60s, represented by Lourdes; and the children of the exile community, represented by Pilar. Three generations of Cuban women tell the story, though Pilar is the overarching narrator. The novel is replete with Afro-Cuban practices that have seeped into the consciousness of both Cubans and Cuban-Americans. The fragmentation of the novel mirrors the fragmentation of Cuban existence, hovering between the Cuba of the past and the Cuban-American present.

In *Dreaming in Cuban*, the manner in which popular religiosity, specifically Afro-Cuban religiosity, functions, varies. Celia, the grandmother, rejects Afro-Cuban practices as witchcraft. At the same time, however, the reader discovers that she visits a *santera* (Afro-Cuban religious priestess and healer) to cure her heartache and that of her son. Her daughter Felicia, who remains with her in Cuba, fully embraces Afro-Cuban religiosity. Her involvement in Afro-Cuban religion grows from spiritual consultations and minor rituals to full initiation into an Afro-Cuban religion. Our first introduction to Felicia is her involvement in an Afro-Cuban ritual to make peace with the spirit of her dead father. Her life ends shortly after her initiation into a *casa de santera* (house of worship for Afro-Cuban religion). Her sister Lourdes does not practice any Afro-Cuban rituals, yet the ghost of her dead father visits her nightly. Thus her story includes an element of the supernatural.

Pilar, who represents the new generation of Cuban-Americans, dabbles in Afro-Cuban practices. As a child she was seen as bewitched by her nannies, who constantly quit after only days of caring for her. Pilar struggles with her identity as a young adult and with her mother's exile politics. Her angst finally leads her to a *botánica*, where she is told that she is a daughter of Changó and must perform a ritual for clarity. This visit to a shop where one purchases supplies for Afro-Cuban religious practices (where she is informed that she should serve under a particular *orisha*, Changó) radically changes her. Though it is her first time engaging in any sort of Afro-Cuban religiosity, she finds a clarity of mind at the end of the ritual she is told to perform that evaded her throughout the novel. The ritual is directly linked to that peace of mind.

The religious practices described by García involve Roman Catholic and African elements. The gods are always African, yet materials used in the rituals, as well as the prayers chanted, are Roman Catholic. Her detailed description of initiation into Afro-Cuban religion demonstrates García's knowledge of these practices. The characters in the novel are dominated by the will of the gods and the spiritual realm. Even Celia acquiesces to allow Felicia to be buried as a *santera* to appease the gods. Lourdes' actions are dominated by the advice of her dead father who visits her nightly. The use of Afro-Cuban rituals is a mark of García's work. García demonstrates their significance for understanding the Cuban and Cuban-American contexts. These syncretic practices form part of Latina spirituality. They demonstrate those gray areas where other religious and faith traditions have become incorporated into Latina beliefs and practices, the traces of the indigenous and African cultures that still remain part of the contemporary Latina context. I realize they may be problematic for some, yet the incorporation of other religious or cultural traditions is not exclusive to Latinas. Also, the inclusion of these practices is not in defiance of Catholic authority; it is merely part of the fabric of Latina culture.

However, not all Latina popular religion falls into this ambiguous realm that some would label syncretism. Overwhelmingly, Latina popular religion remains deeply entrenched within the Roman Catholic tradition. My emphasis on Latinas' popular religion is through examples of three prominent popular religious practices: the Mexican-American celebration of the Day of the Dead, the practice of making *promesas* and home altars. These three rituals highlight the lived religious faith of Latinas and open up new ways of relating to the sacred within Catholic spirituality.

The Day of the Dead

The Mexican-American celebration of the Day of the Dead is a classic example of the importance of family and ancestors for Latinas. The Day of the Dead is usually celebrated on November 1, though in some contexts it is celebrated on November 2 as well. The Day of the Dead has both Aztec and Roman Catholic roots. The Aztec contribution is marked by the presence of food, music, dance and gravesite visits. Aztecs also understood the dead and their ancestors as intercessors between the living and the realm of the supernatural. From the Roman Catholic side comes the tradition of Masses for the dead; the tradition of bringing flowers and food to cemetery visits; the celebration of All Saints and All Souls days; and the belief in the communion of saints. Lara Medina and Gilbert R. Cadena have studied the Day of the Dead celebrations in Los Angeles, and they note that many of the rituals and objects used in the Day of the Dead celebrations have medieval Catholic roots. These include Masses for the dead, flower and food offerings, skull images and the tradition of baking bread on All Souls Day. On the Day of the Dead, families often spend the evening at the graves of their deceased relatives bringing them their favorite foods and drinks. This is a manner of honoring the dead and remaining in communion with them. The bringing of favorite food and drinks to one's deceased family members is a way to affirm their continued presence within the family. Though they have passed away, they are still alive to the families and active participants in the construction of family identity.

The Day of the Dead also reveals a worldview that emphasizes the interconnectedness of life and death. The dead are not gone and departed, they continue to be a part of the present. On the Day of the Dead we remember our ancestors. In a community such as the Mexican-American community in the United States, one whose culture is constantly threatened by the dominant U.S. ethos of assimilation, celebration of this day, and remembering who you are and where you come from is a political and subversive act. However, it is a beautiful ritual that can touch all Catholics. On this day, we remember family members and members of our community who have been significant to our history, our spirituality and our identity. We remind the dead that they have not been forgotten and that they continue to have meaning for us. While not all of us need to spend a day or evening in a cemetery to do this, to set aside time on the Day of the Dead and actively remember our loved ones, perhaps even cooking their favorite dish or doing one of their favorite things, is a wonderful way to make them present to us.

For Mexican-Americans, the Day of the Dead also raises interesting questions about the relationship between popular religion and official religion. It represents an event in which the church is involved but not in charge. Catholics and non-Catholics celebrate side by side. Perhaps the largest celebration of the Day of the Dead occurs in Los Angeles, California. On this day, a large procession fills the streets of Los Angeles. Children and adults have their faces painted as skulls. Many carry marigolds, which are the traditional flowers for altars to the dead. Aztec drums and dancers lead the procession, and often political banners raising Latina issues and struggles dot the street. Catholic churches in East L.A. (which is primarily Latina), such as Dolores Mission, have constructed altars on which are placed pictures of the deceased, marigolds, *pan de muerto* (sweetbread shaped like skulls) and a book of the dead.

Many of the activities surrounding the Day of the Dead involve families, with children, parents and grandparents working together. Women play a prominent role in these activities, especially in the preparation of the *ofrenda* (altarpiece). The skills of the parish altar makers are passed down from mother to daughter, woman to woman. The work they contribute to the church's celebration is a source of pride. The Day of the Dead celebration incorporates not only the traditional Mass, processions and gravesite visits but also poetry, art and dance. Artists have made altar pieces in commemoration of the dead that are displayed in public spaces and galleries throughout East L.A.

The Day of the Dead may resonate with Latinas due, in part, to the practice of *Espiritismo* in Latina communities. *Espiritismo*, or Spiritism, is one of the most widespread religious phenomena in Latin America. It is also one of the least studied. Spiritism is an example of a European religious practice or worldview that has become predominant throughout Latin American cultures as a whole. It is based on a French philosophical and spiritual system that in its origins is understood more as a philosophy than a religion. While its founders saw it as a complementary system to Catholicism, many European sectors of the church deemed it heretical. There are individuals who dabble in Spiritism, while others have formal groups that gather with mediums on a regular basis. They understand their Spiritist activities as entirely Catholic, and they link their practices to rituals such as the Day of the Dead and the communion of saints. The existence of spirits and the special ability some have to channel them is a common belief. Healing plays a prominent role in Spiritism, whether it is the psychological healing that comes through the community gathering of the séance or the physical healing that occurs when one is visited by a spiritual doctor. Spiritism is not exclusive to Latin America and Latinas however, but also has deep roots in New England.

The Catholic church has forcefully condemned Spiritism and its practices. Similarly, the church does not sanction the practice of visiting a *curandera*, or faith healer. Still, faith healing, which is sometimes linked to Spiritism, is a dimension of Latina spirituality in which many Latinas play prominent roles. *Curanderas* who are known for their gift (*don*) of healing are esteemed in a community, and often Latinas turn to them. Many *curanderas* incorporate elements of Catholicism into their healing and rituals. Their ability to heal is seen as a gift from God that must be shared. At the heart of Spiritism is the belief that our deceased loved ones can and do contact us, sometimes through a medium, other times directly. I suspect that Latinas are not alone in this belief. While your spiritual practices may not involve a visit to a medium, and in fact very few Latinas practice Spiritism formally, you may have had the sense of the presence of a deceased loved one in your midst. I am not talking about ghost stories and haunted houses. I refer to feeling the presence and accompaniment of our deceased loved ones.

The Day of the Dead reminds us that death is not the end of our relationship with our loved ones. The Day of the Dead and belief in evil eye in Latina communities open up important conversations on the nature of Roman Catholic religion and the manner in which inculturation shapes and transforms Catholic beliefs and practices. One dimension of the Day of the Dead that I cherish, though it is not my own tradition, is the manner in which humor is incorporated into the remembering of the dead. We see humor in the skeleton outfits, skull masks and figurines that are part of the rituals. To find humor and joy in death and not only sorrow in remembering our deceased loved ones, are lessons I take to heart. The Day of the Dead reminds us that death is not the final word, but anticipates the kingdom of God, when we will be reunited with our loved ones at the end of time.

Promesas

Dear Niño Fidencio,

I would like for you to help me get a job with good pay, benefits, and retirement plan. I promise you if you help me I will make a pilgrimage to your tomb in Espinazo and bring you flowers. Many thanks.[1]

The above prayer represents a *promesa*. A *promesa* is a promise or vow made to a saint, Mary, Jesus or God. Unlike many petitionary or intercessory prayers, *promesas* include some sort of follow-up on the part of the devotee. Part of the petition is therefore the promise to offer a ritual of reverence as a form of gratitude. The gratitude can range from a simple gesture to a grander act. A simple gesture of thankfulness could include candles or flowers placed either at the shrine or home altar of the sacred image to which the petition has been made. A more dramatic thank you might include a pilgrimage or a radical change in the petitioner's behaviors. My friend's Puerto Rican mother, for example, made a petition to Jesus regarding her son, who was born tiny. Worried that he would never grow to an "average" or "acceptable" height as an adult, she promised Jesus she would abstain from eating bread until her son's fifteenth birthday. The abstinence was a sign of her devotion to Jesus and the dire nature of this petition. Sure enough, the son grew to be 5'4", and she resumed her much-missed bread eating at his fifteenth birthday party.

Another example of *promesas*, particularly for Latinas, involves hair. Nancy Pineda-Madrid recounts the story of one of her classmates, Cecilia, who appeared after a Christmas break trip with her knee length hair shorn off. Explaining the haircut, Cecilia explained, "I know. I miss it. But my mom and I had to cut it off because of a *promesa* my mom made to *la Virgen* when I six years old. I guess I never told you. When I was six I got very sick, and the doctors thought that I was going to die. My Mom promised Guadalupe that if I lived she would not cut my hair until I was fourteen. Then, when I turned fourteen, we would cut off my hair and take it to *la Virgen* in thanksgiving for allowing me to live."[2] The *promesa* made by the mother also involved a pilgrimage. Her mother had involved her in the *promesa* as a child, and even though as a young teen she struggled with the haircut, Cecilia honored her mother's promise.

I have a similar *promesa* hanging over me. At the age of thirteen I was in a terrible accident and broke my back. I was hospitalized, placed in a brace and doctors were very unsure if I would ever return to the life I once had prior to the accident. My mother made a *promesa* to Our Lady of Fatima, promising her that she and I would make a pilgrimage to her shrine in Portugal if I recovered. I recovered completely and resumed my life in full health.

Promesas emphasize a dimension of Latina spirituality that I discussed earlier, namely the reciprocal relationship with the sacred. You do not merely offer a prayer. There is also a reciprocal act when that prayer is realized. Central to this is a relational and communal way of understanding our relationships with God, Jesus, Mary and the saints. The sacramental nature of Latina spirituality is also highlighted in a *promesa*. You leave the statue flowers or light a candle, but in fact this is an offering to the particular saint, Mary or image of God. The statue seems to be more than merely an empty image of who it represents; we honor it as we would honor the person it represents. I have always felt like *promesas* are also a "less selfish" way to make a petition. You are not merely asking for something, you are also offering something in return. Sometimes individuals leave little pieces of paper or testimonies of their *promesas* at the altar of a saint or an image of Jesus or Mary. I have visited churches where the image of a saint is literally covered with paper, locks of hair, photos, crutches and war medals. It is a moving sight, and a reminder of the many hopes, struggles and relationships devotees have with the saints, Mary and Jesus.

Home Altars

My mother made our apartment look like a church too: she put a cross with Christ on it over their bed and mine—Papi liked to say that one day it would fall on their heads and kill them.... She hung a picture of the Holy Mother and Baby Jesus on the wall facing my bed, and one of Christ knocking at a door in the hallway. On her dresser she had a painted statue of the Virgin Mary crushing a black snake. When you saw it on the mirror it looked as if she was a real little person who was about to trip over a snake because she wasn't looking where she was going.[3]

Home altars are a common sight in the homes of many Latinas. These altars are the center of a domestic religion which is overwhelmingly female-centered. It is most often the women of the family, either the mother or grandmother, who are in charge of caring for the altar and deciding which saints will inhabit this island of sacred space within the domestic sphere. The presence of a saint often depends on the cultural background of the home. If there is an image of Mary that is part of a home altar, it likely corresponds to their home country. In addition to statues of Mary and the saints, home altars can also include flowers, candles, pictures of deceased loved ones, rosaries, holy water and prayer cards. These small altars, often on dresser tops, chimney mantles and bathroom counters, make the domestic space sacred and are often the heart of home religion.

For Latinas, home altars mark the domestic space as sacred and demonstrate the importance of the sacred in Latina everyday life. They serve as a site of prayer, reflection and remembrance. An example of one saint that appears in many Latina home altars is Saint Martin de Porres. Martin was born in 1579 in Peru. His father, Don Juan de Porres, was Spanish, and his mother, Ana Velázquez, was a freed black slave. Don Juan, while not acknowledging his son (thus rendering him illegitimate) set him up with an apprenticeship with a barber, Dr. Marcelo de Riero of Lima. Martin learned the medical arts and became renown for his healing. At the age of eleven, Martin became a *donado* (a lay helper who received room and board) with the Dominican friars in the Convento del Santo Rosario. In 1603, against social convention, he became a lay brother. Saint Martin became known for his healing powers and his work with marginalized peoples. Throughout Lima he was recognized for his skill in healing; his social work among widows, orphans and prostitutes; his founding of hospitals and orphanages; his work with the poor and racially marginalized of the city; and for his love of animals. He established an orphanage, a children's hospital and an animal shelter. He is referred to today as the "Saint Francis of the Americas." Martin died in 1639 and became the first biracial saint to be canonized in 1962. Because of his healing skills, petitions are often made to him when someone in the family is ill. His statue is also given as a gift to someone who is ill as a sign of protection.

Latinas' relationships with their home altars mirror their real life relationships—dialogical and reciprocal. If you make and receive a petition to a certain saint, you might offer special flowers, light candles or even make a pilgrimage to that saint's shrine. However, if a petition is not granted, the opposite is the case. The petitioner might remove flowers, candles and other offerings. In extreme cases, a statue may be turned upside down or even removed from an altar and placed in a closet. While this may seem irreverent, it in fact demonstrates how intimately Latinas understand their relationships with their home altars and the saints that inhabit them. It is as though these statues are not mere statues; the saints themselves are present in them. This back and forth, give and take relationship with their images reveals Latinas' sacramental worldview. Their relationship with their saints and Mary is also refreshingly unhierarchical and more like a friendship. In an age in which the dangers of hierarchical understandings of the sacred have been shown to promote hierarchical relationship among human beings, a more egalitarian, friendship-based model is a much-needed alternative.

In my own home altar I have various saints that represent my cultural and religious background. Since I am Cuban-American, the centerpiece is unsurprisingly *La Caridad del Cobre.* Saint Barbara, a very popular saint in Cuba, also inhabits my altar space. An image of Saint Martin de Porres that was given to me after I broke my back is also there, as is an image of Our Lady of Fatima, representing the *promesa* my mother made. My grandmother's statue of Saint Clare has a privileged place, for this statue represents a strong devotion on my grandmother's side and one of the few things she brought to the States when she left Cuba. I also have an image of Guadalupe. There are various rosaries, prayer cards, candles, holy water and my grandmother's Latin missal from Cuba. In this altar you find not only my spirituality, but also my story. The objects whisper of my parents' hasty departure from Cuba, the accident that almost took my life. Each rosary has its own personal narrative. Looking at my altar you learn about my culture, my background and my faith. It is not a very big altar and it is crammed on top of a bookshelf, but telling its story is telling my story. In a sense, my altar is symbolic of the larger value and meaning behind popular religious practices. They are the ways in which we, and here I mean all of us, link our stories and our faith. These rituals and objects embody our spirituality and our struggles, both individual and communal.

FOOD FOR THOUGHT

1. How do family members and loved ones who have passed away influence your spirituality?
2. Are there any "unofficial" elements in your spirituality? Do you have feelings of guilt associated with them? How might you sort this out?
3. What saints are important to you and why?

PRAYER FOR EVERYDAY FAITH

Invocation:

> Loving Spirit, guide us.
> Wise Spirit, teach us.
> Just Spirit, empower us.

Reading: Excerpts from Sandra Cisneros, "Little Miracles, Kept Promises," found in her book *Women Hollering Creek and Other Stories*

Response: Let us remember that God encounters us in the everyday.
Loving Spirit, find us.
Let us remember our ancestors and loved ones.
Loving Spirit, accompany us.
Let us feel the presence of the saints as they pray for us.
Loving Spirit, remember us.

CHAPTER FIVE

• THE *VIA CRUCIS* •

The crowd gathers outside the cathedral and in the streets of San Antonio.
The plaza in front of the cathedral is full, and crowds line the surrounding streets. Dolores sees a dark-haired man dressed in a small sheet. He
is carrying a heavy cross, the weight clearly a strain on him. She watches
as the man is tortured and tormented. The crowd yells and screams,
taunting him to continue his journey. A man who looks like her uncle
is dressed in Roman military garb. As he lashes out at the man, Dolores
realizes that it *is* her uncle, yet he is not acting at all like he usually does.
He is someone else.

"Es Jesús" her mother whispers in her ear, as the man walks by
them. "El está sufriendo por nosotros y con nosotros." They follow him
through the streets of downtown. Dolores is confused. She thought
they only celebrated Jesus in the church building and at home. Now it
seems like the city has become a church; all the traffic is stopped, and
they process through the streets freely. She watches the monsignor take
the cross from Jesus and carry it for him. He seems so humble, so unlike
the daunting man preaching at the front of the church every Sunday.

Dolores is overwhelmed by the screams, the sobs and the passion
of the moment. As the soldiers nail Jesus to the cross (the nails are actually fake, her mother assures her, but to Dolores they look very real),
tears well in her eyes. She sees the pain Jesus experiences. She hears the
pain in the people around her: a mother lamenting a son murdered in
a gang-fight last year, a man muttering about his lost job, a young

woman praying her boyfriend will return. Dolores realizes that since they are all with him, Jesus is not suffering alone. She also realizes that because he suffered, they do not suffer alone. He accompanies them all in the daily sufferings of the struggle that is life.[1]

Good Friday

The Jesus of Good Friday is a central representation of Jesus within Latina spirituality. This stems from a theological worldview that strongly emphasizes Jesus' humble origins, his prophetic message and his active presence in the lives of Christians, in particular, his solidarity with the oppressed and marginalized. This strong emphasis on Jesus' suffering and passion distinguishes Latinas from other Catholic ethnic groups in the United States. As noted by Roberto S. Goizueta, "If, among Euro-Americans, nominal Catholics are referred to as 'Christmas and Easter Catholics,' their U.S. Hispanic counterparts are often called 'Ash Wednesday and Good Friday Catholics.'"[2] Latinas identify Jesus as a savior who not only suffers for them but also suffers with them. Latina devotion to the crucified Jesus cannot be found in the dogmas, official teachings or theological treatises of academic theology but instead is situated in the concrete faith and lives of Latina communities. The popular faith expressions of Latina communities play a fundamental role in Latina understandings of Jesus. The suffering of the communal Body of Christ is at the center of this Latina Jesus, seen primarily in the suffering of the oppressed, who continue to bear the pain of the Crucifixion.

Goizueta holds that the foundation of the crucified Christ of Latina popular Catholicism is found in a relational anthropology that sees the human, and consequently Jesus, as essentially social in nature. The image of the *Via Crucis*, which opened this chapter, exemplifies this point.

In the *Via Crucis*, Latinos and Latinas affirm the truth of the Resurrection not as an event that, subsequent to the Crucifixion, "overcomes" or "cancels out" the death of Jesus, but as the inexstinguishable love and solidarity that defines the *Via Crucis* itself, as the act of "accompaniment" that constitutes and empowers us as persons and as a community of faith.[3]

The Latina emphasis on the Crucifixion is not over against the Resurrection but is instead the active, communal confrontation of suffering. As they accompany Jesus to the cross on Good Friday, Latinas affirm the communal nature of our humanity and the promise of life in the face of suffering and death. The emphasis on suffering found on Good Friday is always made with the Resurrection in mind. Latinas accompany Jesus in his suffering knowing that ultimately it is he who will accompany them in their struggles to overcome their suffering. The joy of the Resurrection reminds us that suffering does not have the last word. The final word will be the glorious resurrection.

The *Via Crucis* is a central dimension of Latina devotion to the crucified Christ. While this solemn Good Friday ritual may seem to the outsider like merely a drama, play or simple reenactment, it is not. Through the reenactment, the community is reliving Jesus' suffering, torture and crucifixion. It is happening in the here and now. On this day, the community accompanies Jesus, just as he has accompanied them through their struggles and trials. The *Via Crucis* emerges in response to a community's suffering and raises awareness of the various social, economic and political struggles Latina peoples encounter daily. As noted by anthropologist Karen Mary Davalos in her study of the *Via Crucis* in the predominantly Mexican-American Pilsen neighborhood of Chicago, the *Via Crucis* is a way of uniting the community and promoting lay leadership within the parish through the planning and carrying out of this ritual.

Women Weep

There are various features of the *Via Crucis* that reveal key dimensions of Latina spirituality. The first is the centrality of Mary in Christ's Passion and her significance for Latinas. As Davalos notes in her study of Pilsen, "In fact the women with whom I spoke consistently talked about seeing themselves through Mary's suffering. Although the *Via Crucis* commemorates the death of Jesus, women find particular meaning for their lives as mothers because Pilsen's enactment of the Passion offers them a culturally familiar form and face for their prayers."[4] Representing Mary as a Mexican-American woman leads to a more intimate association with Mary and the Passion events. The women in the community who are mothers identify with Mary's struggles and the deep loss of her son.

I witnessed such identification firsthand when I helped organize the Good Friday rituals at St. Leander parish in San Leandro, California. As part of their Good Friday liturgy, the community places the body of Jesus on a side altar after he is lowered from the cross (the body is a mannequin, not a live actor) and a woman assuming the role of Mary goes to sit with and mourn her dead son alone. Members of the congregation then line up to offer condolences to Mary. As I stood to the side watching this event unfold, I was amazed to see that it was the woman who was playing Mary who was in fact offering the majority of condolences to the Latinas who lined up to hug her. Tears flowed, bodies were wracked with sobs as women repeatedly whispered stories of poverty, wayward husbands and struggles with their children. Though this woman was Martha, whom they knew from their everyday lives and with whom they would probably not so easily share their most personal struggles, at the moment she was not Martha, she was Mary, the mother of Jesus who had just watched her son die and now mourned next to his lifeless body. The word *reenactment* does not adequately summarize what happens in this encounter. On Good Friday, Jesus is crucified again, the community witnesses this and they actively suffer with him and his loved ones.

Within the Latina spirituality of the *Via Crucis* not only Mary, but also the women of Jerusalem who suffer with her, take center stage. Participants make a connection between the suffering of these women centuries ago and their own suffering in their everyday lives. Mary and the women of Jerusalem are a source of strength and empowerment. Like Mary and the other women who watched helplessly as Jesus suffered and died, the women of Pilsen also at times feel paralyzed by the suffering of their families and loved ones. The ritual also creates a moment in which Latinas share leadership roles in the parish and have a decision-making role in ecclesial ritual. This is a space where women's lay leadership flourishes. They are part of the planning process, the organization and the carrying out of the *Via Crucis*.

The Crucified Christ

The *Via Crucis* also helps Latinas transmit their heritage and their culture to future generations of Latinas. As a tradition with deep roots in Latin America, the celebration of the *Via Crucis* is simultaneously a celebration of Latina culture and identity. The affirmation of Latina culture and identity is always at the center of Latina spirituality but perhaps even more so during the *Via Crucis*. One must remember that the *Via Crucis* is a public ritual which occurs in part outside the walls of the church. Processions can have hundreds or even thousands of participants. Part of the *Via Crucis* is the sanctification of public space. Through the *Via Crucis*, the secular public streets of a community become sacred space. The city becomes a church. For Latinas this is especially significant, given efforts to downplay and often criticize Latina cultural practices. Participants in the *Via Crucis* are well aware that when they enter the streets of the city, they are entering the Anglo public space of the dominant culture. The entry of the *Via Crucis* into the streets challenges the ownership of this space and at least for those hours, makes it their own.

While Mary and the Jerusalem women are fundamental for the Latina spirituality of the *Via Crucis*, one cannot downplay the significance of the crucified Christ. I also want to say a word about the heavy emphasis on suffering that surrounds the spirituality of Good Friday. Feminist theologians from around the globe have written passionately about the theme of suffering in our understandings of Jesus and the manner in which it can encourage and legitimize the suffering and abuse of women. Telling women to suffer like Jesus or Mary can be a way to keep women submissive and passive. I am well aware of these insights and take them seriously. On the one hand the glorification of Jesus' suffering can be a way of oppression, a way to maintain a community as meek, humble and submissive. On the other hand, such rituals point to redemptive suffering in which Jesus' and Mary's suffering does not subordinate women but gives them strength in their darkest hours. It is this redemptive suffering that is operative in authentic Latina spirituality. Here women find strength to continue to struggle and survive because they know that even in their darkest, most isolated hours, they do not suffer alone. This does not mean that an emphasis on redemptive suffering cannot lead to a more abusive model of suffering. However, it would be wrong to discount the significance of the cross and redemptive suffering within Latina spirituality as merely a masochistic glorification of suffering.

The Latina devotion to the crucified Jesus and their participation in the *Via Crucis* signals their strong devotion to a crucified Jesus who accompanies them in their suffering. They in turn accompany Jesus on Good Friday. Once again, we see the centrality of reciprocity and community at the center of Latina spiritual devotion. On Good Friday Latinas "return the favor" to Jesus, Mary and the women of Jerusalem, showing them that they do not suffer alone. Latinas also offer the wider Catholic community a dynamic model of spirituality. Through their reenactments of Jesus' Crucifixion, Latinas embrace a sacramental spirituality in which, on Good Friday, Jesus is crucified yearly, his suffering is remembered and the community is re-membered (reunited) in its presence before the cross.

FOOD FOR THOUGHT

1. How is the crucified Christ present in your spirituality?
2. How do you know whether an emphasis on Jesus' suffering is redemptive or functions to oppress women?
3. Would you like to participate in a *Via Crucis*? Why or why not? If you have, what was it like?

PRAYER TO JESUS

Invocation:

> Loving God, accompany us.
> Suffering Servant, remember us.
> Crucified Savior, walk with us.

Scripture: Excerpts from the Passion narrative (for example, Mark 15—16)

Response: Let us pray to Jesus, God's loving Son, who always accompanies us.
Suffering Servant, stand by us.
Let us pray to Jesus, who suffers for us and with us.
Suffering Servant, guide us.
Let us walk with Jesus, our crucified Savior.
Suffering Servant, lead us.

• STRUGGLE AND CELEBRATION:
A SPIRITUALITY OF EVERYDAY LIFE •

Central to Latina spirituality are the struggles that Latinas encounter in their everyday lives. Through their spiritual practices, Latinas are able to express and denounce those oppressive forces which deny their full humanity. In their prayers to Mary and the saints and in their walking with the crucified Jesus, Latinas are reminded that they do not suffer alone. The apparition stories of *virgenes* such as Guadalupe and *La Caridad* reveal an encounter with the sacred that accompanies the oppressed. These stories also remind Latinas that the divine's message often comes in unlikely forms through unexpected voices. These moments that condemn suffering and injustice, however, are also moments of celebration. Whether it is the humor of the Day of the Dead, the *fiesta* that often accompanies the feast day celebrations of saints or the reminder that the Resurrection always follows the Crucifixion, Latina spirituality does not give suffering and struggle the final word. Through their committed social action, Latinas call others into the struggle against injustice. The justice-infused nature of Latina spirituality invites others into the struggle against oppression, calling you to find your struggle, your passion and your concrete Christian commitment.

The commitment to the struggle, as the title of this text implies, is also a moment of celebration. My students often complain to me that in highlighting the injustices of the world, my course can seem like a downer. I usually retort that if that is the case, then they are only getting half the message. While highlighting injustice and oppression can be depressing, engaging in the struggle against that injustice can be a source of joy and celebration. As Ada María Isasi-Díaz has reminded us, to walk in the picket line is a prayerful moment; it is an instance of joy and celebration. These moments of celebration can be communal and individual, organized or spur-of-the-moment.

Creative rituals, such as the Guadalupe reenactment or the ritual that concludes this reflection on Latina spirituality, are moments of celebration that are spiritually nourishing and liberating. Through the incorporation of stories of women who are forgotten—women who have contributed to our spiritual lives but who do not make it into the great narratives of Christian history—these rituals provide a more inclusive celebration of Catholic spirituality. However, our everyday moments are equally important. Whether it is my morning cup of coffee that I savor, knowing that a Catholic parish is providing fair wages for the men, women and children who pick the beans or lighting a candle to a statue with a quick prayer—these everyday moments of spiritual celebration feed our spiritual lives.

The focus of this volume on community and communion represents the significance of both the community/family *as noun* and the coming together in community *as verb* that is so central to Latina spirituality. Community and family are not only a large part of Latina identity as static aspects of our heritage, they are an active dimension of our faith life when we come together. This sense of community and family reaches out to our extended families, our neighbors, our ancestors, those with whom we worship, laugh and cry. This community includes Jesus, Mary and the saints.

It is fitting therefore, to conclude with a ritual that highlights the community of women who are important to Latina Catholic spirituality. I offer suggestions about how you might shape this ritual. Through the naming of the women in your particular life who have influenced your spirituality, we aim to expand this community to bear witness to all the women who have touched our spiritual lives. The incorporation of food in this ritual, the sharing of a meal, is a "communion" with the smells and tastes of our heritages, our souls.

The practice of altar building in this ritual reminds us of the importance of home altars for Latinas, where their friends the saints and their deceased loved ones remain an ever-present aspect of their spirituality. I also suspect that many of the women who participate in this ritual will carry with them a representation of their spiritual lives. Whether it is a prayer card or statue in one's purse, a photo or a piece of jewelry, the different ways that we carry our spirituality around with us bear witness to the sacredness of everyday life. In fact, it is often an object that represents the most precious dimension of our spirituality that accompanies us, sometimes out of sight, during work, school and those mundane tasks that fill our free moments. This "Latina" emphasis on the everyday, therefore, is not exclusive to us, yet serves as a reminder of the ways in which we all encounter and cherish the sacred in our everyday lives. I am often wary that when I approach a subject as a Latina or on behalf of Latinas that my words will be sidelined as pertaining only to a particular group or culture. I hope I have communicated that the richness of Latina spirituality can be a source for *all* Catholic women and that you have connected to the communal, joyous spirituality that Latinas share, finding celebration amidst the struggle and finding the sacred in the everyday.

Closing Ritual

Throughout this text we have traveled through the world of Latina spirituality, highlighting how Latinas understand and relate to the sacred. As a way of ending this journey, I offer the following ritual to be done in community. If you wish, you could also do an abridged, more personal version of this ritual on your own.

The Environment

A ritual that emphasizes the spirituality, lives and struggles of Latinas must take seriously the sacred spaces that Latinas often create in their homes and personal spaces. One manifestation of that space is the home altar. Therefore, the liturgical space should have an altar in the center with various elements that constitute Latina spirituality: statues of the various manifestations of Mary in Latin American countries, saints favored by Latinas, crucifixes, rosaries and candles. Because the art of weaving is one way that many Latinas and Latin American women express themselves (indigenous women in particular), a hand-woven cloth should be placed under the altar. Ritual participants should also bring an object (a prayer card, statue, photograph) of a woman who represents a central dimension of their spirituality. The ritual should be led by at least two women in order to offer a model of communal, shared leadership.

Call to Worship

The call to worship involves singing a hymn or song, preferably bilingual, and should draw upon whatever theme the participants wish to emphasize. The companion CD to this series offers some good choices. Also, the *Flor y Canto* hymnal is an excellent resource.

Scripture Reading: The Samaritan Woman: John 4:4–42

Homily

One or two of the worship leaders should now lead the group in a shared reflection on the biblical passage and its significance for Latina spirituality. Some questions that could guide the discussion are:

- What is your initial reaction to the biblical story?
- How does Jesus' speaking to the Samaritan woman challenge us to reach out to those marginalized communities in our midst? Remember, Samaritans were considered impure by most Jews.
- When have you acted like the disciples, judging someone based on their race, ethnicity or gender? Can you acknowledge this failure and

open yourself to God's gracious forgiveness?

• What does it mean for Jesus to empower this woman to spread the gospel message?

A Litany of Latinas, Latin American and Biblical Women

We remember Hagar, the Egyptian slave and surrogate, whose struggles remind us that women are among the most oppressed of peoples, and that we must be attentive to how gender, race and class shape our relationships and spirituality.

We remember the Hebrew midwives in the Exodus story, Shiphrah and Puah, who risked their lives in order to contribute to the liberation of the enslaved Hebrew people.

We remember the unnamed women in Judges 19, who remind us of the thousands of unnamed Latinas who suffer violence and abuse in silence.

We remember Mary, the Mother of God, who lifted the lowly in her Magnificat and offered her son as a model of social justice and a preferential option for the poor.

We remember Mary Magdalene, who offers us a model of discipleship that all Christians should emulate.

We remember La Malinche, Cortés translator and concubine, who was forced into servitude like so many other indigenous women during the conquest and even today.

We remember Sor Juana Inés de la Cruz, an intellectual foremother who teaches us about Latinas' contribution to the theology of the church.

We remember Dolores Huerta, whose support of the United Farm Workers offers a model of grassroots leadership in the struggle.

We remember all the unnamed Latina mothers and *abuelitas*, who struggle silently for their families and their communities.

"Communion" Ceremony

Worship organizers might prepare foods that represent the diversity of Latina culture. Or the group might mix traditional Latina foods with dishes that represent food from different cultural backgrounds. Two or three women might bring the dishes to the altar and offer a prayerful reflection on how this food contributes to the spiritual life of the women present.

Altar Building

All of the women are invited to bring forth whatever sacred object they have with them. They should describe their object and its significance, highlighting how it represents their strength and spirituality. Instrumental music should accompany this segment of the ritual.

Closing Reflection

The worship leader or leaders offer some closing reflection and then invite the ritual participants to share in the "communion" of foods present on the altar.

CHAPTER ONE

1. Ada Maria Isasi-Díaz, "Elements of a Mujerista Anthropology," in *Mujerista Theology: A Theology for the Twenty-First Century* (Maryknoll, N.Y.: Orbis, 1996), p. 128.

2. Sor Juana Inés de la Cruz, *The Answer/La Respuesta: Including a Selection of Poems*, Electa Arenal and Amanda Powell, critical ed. and trans. (New York: CUNY, 1994), p. 75.

CHAPTER TWO

1. Sheila Cosminsky, "Guatemala: The Evil Eye in a Quiché Community," in *The Evil Eye*, Clarence Maloney, ed. (New York: Columbia University Press, 1976), pp. 163–172.

2. Orlando O. Espín, "Tradition and Popular Religion: An Understanding of the *Sensus Fidelium*," in *The Faith of the People: Theological Reflections on Popular Catholicism* (Maryknoll, N.Y.: Orbis, 1997), pp. 65–66.

3. Pope John Paul II, "Address to the Pontifical Academy of Social Sciences," April 2001, no. 2.

CHAPTER THREE

1. Nancy Pineda-Madrid, "Traditioning: The Formation of Community, the Transmission of Faith," in *Futuring Our Past: Explorations in the Theology of Tradition*, Orlando O. Espín and Gary Macy, eds. (Maryknoll, N.Y.: Orbis, 2006), p. 207.

2. Sandra Cisneros, "Guadalupe the Sex Goddess," in *Goddess of the Americas: Writings on the Virgin of Guadalupe*, Ana Castillo, ed. (New York: Riverhead, 1996), p. 48.

3. Cisneros, p. 51.

CHAPTER FOUR

1. Cisneros, "Little Miracles, Kept Promises," in *Women Hollering Creek and Other Stories* (New York: Vintage Contemporaries, 1992), p. 118.

2. Pineda-Madrid, p. 206.

3. Judith Ortiz Cofer, "By Love Betrayed," in *The Latin Deli: Telling the Lives of Barrio Women* (New York: Norton, 1993), p. 25.

CHAPTER FIVE

1. Michelle A. Gonzalez, "Vignette," in *Constructive Theology: A Contemporary Approach to Classical Themes*, Serene Jones and Paul Lakeland, eds. (Minneapolis: Fortress, 2005), pp. 161–162.

2. Goizueta, "A Matter of Life and Death: Theological Anthropology Between Calvary and Galilee," *CTSA Proceedings* 53 (1998), pp. 2–3.

3. Goizueta, p. 3.

4. Karen Mary Davalos, " 'The Real Way of Praying:'The Via Crucis, *Mexicano* Sacred Space, and the Architecture of Domination," in *Horizons of the Sacred: Mexican Traditions in U.S. Catholicism*, Timothy Matovina and Gary Riebe-Estrella, eds. (Ithaca, N.Y.: Cornell University, 2002), p. 50.

Books

Aquino, María Pilar. *Our Cry for Life: Feminist Theology from Latin America* (Maryknoll, N.Y.: Orbis, 1993). An excellent introduction to the spirituality and struggles of Latinas and Latina American women.

Castillo, Anna, ed. *Goddess of the Americas: Writings on the Virgin of Guadalupe* (New York: Riverhead, 1996). This book offers a variety of interpretations of Guadalupan spirituality and its impact on Latinas and Latin Americans.

Cisneros, Sandra. *Women Hollering Creek and Other Stories* (New York: Vintage, 1992). A delightful source for tapping into the religious imagination of Latinas.

Cofer, Judith Ortiz. *The Line of the Sun* (Athens, Ga.: University of Georgia Press, 1989). A wonderful, spiritually nourishing novel.

Elizondo, Virgilio, ed., John Drury, trans. *Way of the Cross: The Passion of Christ in the Americas* (Oxford: Rowan and Littlefield, 2002). This book offers a profound spiritual meditation on the *Via Crucis* from the perspective of the poor of the Americas.

García, Cristina. *Dreaming in Cuban* (New York: Ballantine, 1993).

Goizueta, Roberto S. *Caminemos Con Jesús: A Hispanic/Latino Theology of Accompaniment* (Maryknoll, N.Y.: Orbis, 1995). An analysis of the *Via Crucis* procession in San Antonio, Texas, opens this book.

Isasi-Díaz, Ada María. *En la Lucha / In the Struggle: Elaborating a Mujerista Theology* (Minneapolis: Fortress, 1993). An excellent introduction to the spirituality and struggles of Latinas and Latina American women.

John Paul II. *Ecclesia in America*. This document represents an important moment in the church's self-understanding as a truly "American Church."

Rodríguez, Jeanette. *Our Lady of Guadalupe: Faith and Empowerment Among Mexican-American Women* (Austin: University of Texas Press, 1994). Focuses on Mexican-American women's Guadalupan spirituality.

———. *Stories We Live / Cuentos Que Vivimos* (New York: Paulist, 1996). A wonderful book on Latinas' cultural memory in relation to their spirituality.

Schreiter, Robert. *The New Catholicity: Theology Between the Global and Local* (Maryknoll, N.Y.: Orbis, 1997). An important study on the impact of globalization on Catholicism.

Villanseñor, Victor. *Rain of Gold* (New York: Delta, 1991). A classic literary epic of the Mexican-American experience.

I also recommend reading the lives of the particular saints who are significant within your own cultural background.

Other Media

Bordertown, Gregory Nava's most recent picture, starring Jennifer Lopez, examines the murder of hundreds of women on the U.S.-Mexican border. This is a fictionalized account of the real-life wave of murders of young factory women in the Juarez area of Mexico.

Yo, La Peor de Todas (1995) An Argentinian film directed by María Luisa Bemberg, that is a wonderful depiction of the life and struggles of Sor Juana Inés de la Cruz.

El Norte (1983) A powerful film on Guatemalan illegal immigrants' journey to the United States in order to escape military persecution in their home country. Directed by Gregory Nava.

Artists Alma Lopez (www.almalopez.net) and Yolanda Lopez (www.yolandalopez.net) have excellent Web sites displaying their Guadalupan art.

The Called to Holiness Web site offers articles, reviews and author interviews. Please visit it at www.CalledtoHoliness.org.

Called to Holiness Series

A groundbreaking eight-volume series on women's spirituality, *Called to Holiness: Spirituality for Catholic Women* will cover the many diverse facets of a woman's interior life and help her discover how God works with her and through her. An ideal resource for a woman seeking to find how God charges the moments of her life—from spirituality itself, to the spirituality of social justice, the spirituality of grieving the loss of a loved one, the creation and nurturing of families, the mentoring of young adult Catholic women, to recognition of the shared wisdom of women in the middle years—this series can be used by individuals or in groups. Far from the cloister or monastery, these books find God in the midst of a woman's everyday life and help her to find and celebrate God's presence day to day and acknowledge her own gifts as an ordinary "theologian." The books can be used independently or together for individual discussion or group faith sharing. Each book will include gathering rituals, reflection questions and annotated bibliographies.

Living a Spirituality of Action
A Woman's Perspective

Joan Mueller

"Own your gifts and use them to make the world a better place," Catholic theologian Joan Mueller writes. In this practical book she provides us with ideas and encouragement to live and act with courage to change the world, even if our actions are sometimes small.

This is a book for all who hear about hungry people living in the park and decide to make sandwiches, who volunteer to teach children to read, who raise money to change systems that provide substandard care to the vulnerable, who can imagine a mothered world. Mueller invites us to discuss and embrace our shared wisdom.

Release: August 2008
Religion — Spirituality
Paper, 112 pp.
Order #B16885
ISBN 978-0-86716-885-3
$11.95

Called to Holiness Publication Schedule

Fall 2008:
- Making Sense of God:
A Woman's Perspective
(Elizabeth A. Dreyer)
ISBN 978-0-86716-884-6

- Grieving With Grace:
A Woman's Perspective
(Dolores R. Leckey)
ISBN 978-0-86716-888-4

- Living a Spirituality of
Action: A Woman's
Perspective (Joan Mueller)
ISBN 978-0-86716-885-3

Spring 2009:
- Embracing Latina
Spirituality: A Woman's
Perspective
(Michelle A. Gonzalez)
ISBN 978-0-86716-886-0

- Awakening to Prayer:
A Woman's Perspective
(Clare Wagner)
ISBN 978-0-86716-892-1

Fall 2009:
- Creating New Life,
Nurturing Families:
A Woman's Perspective
(Sidney Callahan)
ISBN 978-0-86716-893-8

- Weaving Faith and
Experience: A Woman's
Perspective on the Middle
Years (Patricia Cooney
Hathaway)
ISBN 978-0-86716-904-1

- Finding My Voice:
A Young Adult Woman's
Perspective
(Beth M. Knobbe)
ISBN 978-0-86716-894-5

Called to Holiness Companion CD
Musical selections to accompany the gathering rituals for the book series. Order #A9001 **$19.95**

Grieving With Grace
A Woman's Perspective
Dolores R. Leckey

There are many ways in which the course of our daily lives can be altered—illness, change in residence, loss of employment and death of loved ones. These alterations can require dramatic and even subtle changes in our everyday living, limit our options and force us to choose different priorities.

Dolores Leckey knows firsthand that the death of a spouse changes forever the rhythms of life at all levels—body, mind and soul. In this moving and personal narrative that includes entries from her journal, she shares with us her own shift in consciousness, in the way she sees God, herself and the world after her husband's death. She offers us consolation and hope.

Release: August 2008
Religion — Spirituality
Paper, 112 pp.
Order #B16888
ISBN 978-0-86716-888-4
$11.95

ABOUT THE AUTHOR

Michelle A. Gonzalez, PH.D., is assistant professor of religious studies at the University of Miami. She received her doctorate in systematic and philosophical theology at the Graduate Theological Union in Berkeley, California. She spent two years working with a Mayan community in San Lucas Tolimán, Guatemala. Her research and teaching interests include Latino/a, Latin American and feminist theologies, as well as interdisciplinary work in Afro-Cuban studies. She wrote *Sor Juana: Beauty and Justice in the Americas* and *Afro-Cuban Theology: Religion, Race, Culture and Identity.*